THE
CANNIBAL'S
COOKBOOK

Recipes and Remedies
for Human Sacrifice

BY THE SAME AUTHOR

ISLAND IN SPACE
Prospectus for a New Idea

Editor, and Co-Author with
Carl Sagan, Thor Hyerdahl,
Jacques-Yves Cousteau,
Gwynne Dyer, Donald
Johanson, Richard Leakey,
Robert Muller, Russell
Schweikart, Lewis Thomas
and Alvin Toffler.

A global blueprint published
by the United Nations. More
than twenty-five thousand
copies sold.
ISBN 0-920-417-57-4

ABOUT THE AUTHOR

Dr. Pamela Peck is a Cultural Anthropologist whose professional interest is education for a global perspective and the application of Social Science knowledge to the practical concerns of everyday life. Canadian born, she has received the degrees of Bachelor of Arts in Psychology (Mount Allison University), Bachelor of Social Work, Master of Social Work and Doctor of Philosophy in Anthropology (University of British Columbia). She was a Research Associate at the University of Delhi (India) and a Research Fellow at the University of the South Pacific (Fiji). Awards include doctoral fellowships from the University of British Columbia, the Canada Council and the International Development Research Centre. She was also a Killam Post-Doctoral Fellow.

Dr. Peck has visited, lived and worked in more than forty countries, and assignments have included concept development and scripting for United Nations pavilions at two world expositions. As a writer, speaker and counsellor, she demonstrates how culture shapes our perceptions of reality, and offers a means of critical insight into and freedom from the constraints of the "social" world.

Like Margaret Mead before her, Dr. Pamela Peck travelled to the South Pacific to undertake anthropological fieldwork, and returned to share her ideas and research with University students. And like Dr. Mead, she stretched the boundaries of *academia* to make Anthropology relevant to everyday life. Here are a few of the comments students of all ages have made about her and her teaching:

> *"She has a fresh new exciting outlook on life."*

> *"Very effective at challenging the rigid mental structures that I operate with. I am happy to undo these now ineffective systems."*

> *"Her knowledge is far-reaching, and her ability to use her knowledge is wonderfully complemented by her compassion and love."*

> *"Her creative approach is exceptional."*

> *"She really opened our minds and our eyes."*

> *"Knows what she is talking about and is able to present it clearly."*

> *"She's very inspiring."*

> *"Concise, entertaining, stimulating and understanding."*

> *"My mind continues to see (and see through) new things from what she's taught me."*

> *"Pam is able to clearly explain in a logical way that which surpasses logic and rationalism."*

"She has a great ability to provoke thought about our own culture and the part Anthropology can play in every-day life."

"She has helped us to look at institutions in society with a critical eye."

"She stimulated us to think critically and independently."

"She broadened my horizons magnifi-cently."

"She provided a real opportunity to see things in a new way."

"Very interesting...helpful, understanding, funny."

"She made me look at my own life and think about it, and about the way I live it."

"Dr. Peck was able to get me to think and question things that, for me, was an education in itself."

"...a course in life...that I can actually apply to my own life."

"She gave me a new insight on life."

"She provided the path to greater under-standing."

"Stimulating and captivating."

"Good sense of humour."

"Enlightening."

Dedicated to the more than five billion of us who share the bounty of planet Earth, and to those yet to come—so that we may all have life and have it abundantly.

THE CANNIBAL'S COOKBOOK

Recipes and Remedies for Human Sacrifice

Pamela Peck, Ph.D.

PJenesis Press

Copyright © 1996 by Pamela J. Peck

Published by:

PJenesis Press
City Square
Post Office Box 47105
Vancouver Canada V5Z 4L6

First printing, 1996.

Canadian Cataloguing in Publication Data

Peck, Pamela J. (Pamela Janice), 1944-
  The Cannibal's Cookbook

ISBN 0-9699895-0-4

1. Culture. 2. Anthropology--Psychological aspects. 3. Self.
I. Title.
HM101.P42 1996   306   C95-910866-1

Contributing Editor: Ken Johnson
Cover Design and illustrations: Pamela J. Peck
Typesetting and design: PJenesis Press
Printed in Canada on recycled paper with non-petroleum ink.

CONTENTS

PART II: **RECIPES FOR HUMAN SACRIFICE (ctd)**

PART III: **TIME TO TAKE STOCK** 179

PART IV: **ENTERTAINING IDEAS** 193

PART V: **THE DINNER PARTY** 209

NOTES 216

BIBLIOGRAPHY 220

"FOREWARNED"

This book is built around some stories that will take you on a global—indeed, cosmic—adventure. You might even "lose your self" in here! So let me tell you something about the layout, to help you find your way through its many passages.

Part I of the book—The Art of Cannibal Cookery—is an "appetizer". It's there to put things in perspective, to tell you what cannibalism was and is all about.

Part II is "the main course": thirty "Recipes for Human Sacrifice" which have been collected from cultures around the world. In a stark and poignant way, they "bring home" the age-old adage that truth is stranger than fiction. Some of the stories may shock you, because they reveal rather bizarre aspects of our cultural behaviour. Others may leave you feeling unsettled, because they cut to the core of our beliefs and values. Still others will make you laugh: life is funny sometimes—and laughter is good medicine for the soul.

All thirty "recipes" are short—three or four pages in most cases—and are sufficient unto themselves. But that's not "the whole story", and that's why "the desserts" are there—to get us beyond the constraints of our cultural conditioning so that we might truly experience the joy and wonder of life. Part III unravels the mystery of how culture weaves and binds us in its "spell"; Part IV takes us step by step through the stages of getting "out of bounds"; and Part V offers some "Table Manners" for sharing Earth's bounty, and ends by "Saying Grace".

Now, before you start to read, there are two fundamental things you should know. The first has to do with the book's content; the second, with its form.

With regard to content, it may appear at first glance that I am pronouncing on specific cultural groups—Fijians, Samoans, Egyptians, British, French, Japanese...and that I am singling out individuals who occupy particular roles in society—monarchs, priests, politicians, journalists, athletes, academics.... You might even "find your Self" in here! So let me make it clear at the outset that my critique is not about groups or individuals *per se* but rather about the societies that create them, and the institutions that maintain and reinforce them. Fijian people are wonderful; so are Samoans, Egyptians, British, French and Japanese.... I'm sure the "Queen" is a very nice lady, and that the Pope wants to do "the right thing". The same goes for individual politicians, journalists, athletes and academics; like us, they are just trying to make their lives work. Please keep that in mind.

Now, about the second thing: form. Sometimes you will encounter a familiar word "spelled" in an unfamiliar way. Sometimes a sentence without a verb in it. Not to mention sentences that begin with "not", "and", "so", "but" and "because". Because my goal is to get the point across—to "tell it like it is"; I'm more interested in communicating than in being "grammatically correct".

In the end, *The Cannibal's Cookbook* is my offering of thanks for the rich experiences life has afforded me up to now. I share it in the sincere hope that its "food for thought" will provide nourishment for your soul.

Bon appetit!

Pamela
Vancouver
1996

ACKNOWLEDGMENTS

To my very special friends in Fiji, especially those on the island of Ngau in Lomaiviti, thank-you for sharing your lives and your history.

To the many people around the world—from Egypt to India, from Paris to Papeete—especially those who took me into their homes and villages, thank-you for sharing your culture and your stories.

To my friends and associates at home in Canada, thank-you for sharing your love and your talents. Special thanks go to Ken Johnson for his outstanding work and support as Contributing Editor and Co-publisher, to Randy Ormston for encouraging me to write this book and helping me along the way, to Bill Hanna for planting the brilliant title in my mind, and to Ron Ormston and Barbara Yearsley for copy editing my casual conversational style into (almost) "grammatically correct" English; I could not have done it without you.

Special mention must here be made to the writers and thinkers whose works I have freely used to illuminate the path away from "Cannibal Cookery". (Standard disclaimers apply.) I am especially indebted in Part III to Eric Fromm and in Part IV to Ken Wilber. Anyone familiar with the brilliant writings of these two men will recognize the infusion of their ideas throughout and appreciate the enormous intellectual debt I owe them. I acknowledge the same indebtedness to two other outstanding thinkers, Carl Jung and Jiddu Krishnamurti; they have contributed to my life and work in ways I cannot adequately express. I have listed some principal titles from each of the four in the Bibliography.

And finally, I acknowledge you, the reader. To have picked up this volume and read thus far, you have selected yourself to be among those who care about the quality of life for yourself and others on the planet. Our collective well-being is my goal, and if your life is enhanced even in some small measure by something you discover in these pages, I will feel amply rewarded.

PART I

THE ART OF CANNIBAL COOKERY

CANNIBALISM YESTERDAY AND TODAY

In the latest film version of the mutiny on the *Bounty*—the one with Mel Gibson—there's a scene after the mutiny where Captain Bligh is in his little boat, with his little crew, and their little stores—all three running very low—and he's wondering what to do next. They've already stopped at the island of Tofua from where they've had to make a quick getaway because the natives aren't very friendly.

There they are, drifting westward. They're hungry, they're thirsty, they're exhausted, they're suffering from exposure—and just off the horizon are three hundred and fifty of the lushest and loveliest islands in the whole of the South Pacific. Taro, breadfruit, coconuts, mangos, papayas, fresh water, and a reef full of fish: in short, everything they need to sustain life.

But they can't stop there. Why? Because, cautions the well-seasoned Captain, that lush and lovely archipelago constitutes "the most savage islands in these waters, the Fiji islands, where cannibalism is perfected almost to a science".

A scene or two later, one of his mutinied crew is dying. "When my spirit is gone," he whispers to Bligh, "there will be nothing but the flesh remaining. I beg you, use that poor flesh to save the others." The Captain replies, "No, no, Mr.

Nelson; we're civilized men, not savages, and civilized men we shall die."

There you have it: savage Fijians on the one hand and civilized Englishmen on the other. That parallel intrigues me because both are members of the same species yet they have very different ideas about what it means to be human.

Or do they? Or should I say, did they, because that event took place in 1789. Two centuries later, almost to the year, I am in the Fiji islands. In fact, I'm in that same area where Bligh "sailed on by". It's called Bligh Water now; they named it after him. The island I sail to is Ngau (pronounced "now"). Luckily for him he didn't come here because this is the island in Fiji where cannibalism is said to have originated. Not only that, the cannibals on Ngau further distinguished themselves by cooking the *bokola* whole. (*Bokola* is the name they gave to the dead bodies destined for the cannibal ovens.) In other parts of Fiji, they would dismember the bodies, then cook and serve the parts—but here on Ngau, they served the bodies whole.

> **Bokola** *is the name they gave to the dead bodies destined for the cannibal ovens.*

It was not only the famous Captain Bligh who feared the "savages" of eighteenth century Fiji. Explorers charting the Fijian waters and traders who sailed here in search of sandalwood and *beche de mer* (sea cucumbers) returned home with tales of cannibalism, widow strangling, human sacrifice, murder of the aged and infirm, female infanticide....

Such reports turned more than a few stomachs back in England, and none more so than queasy Christian ones. The Methodist Church got into the act and sent a couple of missionaries. An English historian named Henderson* describes what greeted them. (* See Notes, p. 217)

As might be expected, the missionaries were most deeply impressed, especially at first, by the savage and apparently inhuman atrocities that were practised as a matter of course, sometimes within a stone's throw of their own homes. They saw the *bokola* brought into harbour on canoes, seized by an arm or a leg, and hastily dragged away to the *rara* (open space in the centre of a village), then taken back to the beach, cut up with as much *sang-froid* as a butcher displays in dismembering an ox, and with skill enough to astonish a trained British surgeon. After being cooked, the gods got a share (which the priests and some of the old men eat) and the rest was distributed among the men; but if the supply was large enough the women and children would get a portion.

"The favourite portions were the thigh and upper arm, and the flesh of women and children was preferred to that of men."

Tastes differed, but to many human flesh was a delicacy equal to chicken or turtle. The favourite portions were the thigh and upper arm, and the flesh of women and children was preferred to that of men. It is a mistake to think that Fijians of this period eat only the bodies of their enemies taken in war. Whenever a distinguished chief came from Mbau, and there were no *bokola* in the city, women and children fishing on the reefs would be stalked and taken, dressed and cooked to furnish him with appetizing dishes....

Here's another tidbit.

Slaughtered human bodies were in demand for other purposes than feasting. When a canoe was built, bodies of men were used for rollers in launching it. After it had been launched the decks were smeared with the blood of other victims for good luck and to pay respect to the gods. In building a temple men would be sacrificed to give strength to the posts that supported the structure.

These are just appetizers, by the way. Or should I say "horrid'oeuvres"?

Another custom which harrowed the feelings of the missionaries and their wives was the strangling of widows—and other relatives—on the death of a chief. When remonstrated with, the chiefs would reply that it was their custom and, from their point of view, no further argument was necessary.

And here is yet another little morsel:

No less appalling to the missionaries was the manner in which the old and infirm were treated in Fiji. They were quickly given to understand (where it was needed) that they were a nuisance to their friends and relatives, and that it would be better for them to put an end to their existence. Some of the old folks would go to their death on their own initiative...to a grave in which they sat huddled up while the earth was thrown over them and stomped down by their friends and relatives. Sometimes the poor creatures would plead for a cessation of the stomping, and a few are reported to have begged for a drink of water. But it was useless; on such occasions the community instinct operated with irresistible power.

Then there's the story of a boy from a chiefly clan whose thigh was bitten by a shark.

...relations and friends exchanged views on the subject, and came to the conclusion that it could not be permitted that a (future) chief should be seen going abroad whose leg had been bitten by a shark. He was strangled the same night.

The goal of the missionaries was to save the lost souls of these "savages" by converting them to Christianity. But they met with little success. The natives weren't predisposed toward the new religion; it didn't make sense to them in any case—and they were certainly in no mood to give up the eating of human flesh. Cannibalism remained an esteemed cultural practice among the Fijians, as did widow strangling, human sacrifice, murder of the aged and infirm, and female infanticide.

That's when a missionary by the name of Thomas Williams—only twenty-five years of age—arrived on the scene with his new bride. The year was 1840. I single out this young man because he wrote what became the best and most thorough account of culture in early Fiji. He became my eyes: he saw what I was not there to see. And he saw plenty of cannibalism. "There were many," he wrote,

> who refused to believe in the existence of this horrible practice in modern times; but such incredulity has been forced to yield to indisputable and repeated evidence, of which Fiji alone can supply enough to convince a universe, that man can fall so low as *habitually* to feed upon his fellowmen.**

His accounts are graphic, to be sure, but there were acts so horrendous that Williams could not bring himself to commit them to pen. "I could cite well authenticated instances of such horrors," he writes, "but their narration would be far more revolting than profitable."

What he did record is horrendous enough, and I have included excerpts from his eye witness account at the conclusion of each of the thirty "Recipes" in Part II of this "Cookbook".***

Strange that it would be a missionary among the cannibals of Fiji who would teach me the art of cannibal cookery!

However, that's not the only reason I single out this missionary among the cannibals of Fiji. Thomas Williams did more than just see for me; he "shifted the direction of my look"—not because of what he was able to see in the Fijian culture, but ironically, because of what he was *not* able to see in his own. That *oversight* was, for me, the *eye-opener* on how people can be seduced into taking part in cannibalism, not to mention human sacrifice, widow strangling, murder of the aged and infirm, and female infanticide. Strange that it would be a missionary among the cannibals of Fiji who would teach me the art of cannibal cookery!

Thomas Williams attributed the "lost" condition of the "uncivilized" Fijian to "an underregulated nature". He was wrong. Fijian cannibalism did not spring from an *underregulated nature* but rather from an *overregulated culture*. In other words, it was his table manners, not his lack of grace, that selected the Fijian to be a cannibal. It is the same for us. Indeed, as this "Cookbook" will demonstrate, we do not go very far in an understanding of being "lost" or being "saved" if we cannot read these conditions in the great forces that shape our economic life, our social life, our political life, and our religious life. This is what the missionary failed to see.

The real issue, surely, is not how you treat bodies when they are dead but how you treat human beings when they are alive.

Like most British people—then and now—Thomas Williams prided himself on his cultivated moral taste. This was the same moral taste that was savoured by the famous Captain Bligh—who, by the way, escaped the cannibal ovens of savage Fiji and made his way home to civilized England. Once back in the swing of things, he tracked down some of his mutineers in Tahiti and had them killed—all because they had decided there were things they would rather do than risk their lives taking him around the Horn. And he was able to get away with it because he had the weight of the British Admiralty behind him.

Now is that civilized? Or is it savage? To say a people is civilized or savage on the basis of their eating habits is to express nothing more than a cultural opinion. What's the difference between taking the people you kill and putting them in the ground and burying them, and taking the people you kill and putting them in the oven and eating them? It's just a matter of taste. Ask the Hindus, especially if they are high caste Hindus, and they'll probably tell you the idea of eating the flesh of a cow is revolting. (Some people won't even eat eggs!) Let's face it, a chunk of flesh, once it's dead, is a chunk of flesh. That dying seaman on Bligh's little boat had that one figured out—and he was no cannibal. The real issue, surely, is not how you treat bodies when they are dead but how you treat human beings when they are alive.

As for those "savage" Fijians, they finally "licked the habit" of eating each other. The very year after Thomas Williams departed the archipelago in defeat, the paramount chief of Fiji determined it was in his best interests to convert to Christianity. Put another way, he found himself in urgent need of a few extraneous aids—like guns and ammunition—from the British. The new religion of the paramount chief quickly became the religion of the people: commoners now converted by chiefly decree.

Out went "heathenism"—and out went a good deal of Fijian culture, because you can't have one without the other. In went Christianity—and in went a good deal of European culture, because again, you can't have one without the other. The missionaries did not free the Fijians from the perils of culture. They just freed them from the perils of *Fijian* culture, and introduced them to the perils of *European* culture. They may have removed human flesh from the menu, but they substituted some pretty unsavory recipes of their own.

So after the middle of the nineteenth century, declare the history books, cannibalism disappeared from Fiji. Or did it? I was there after the middle of the twentieth century and I saw plenty of it! Not only in Fiji. I saw it in India too, as well as in Thailand, and Indonesia, and in Egypt, France, the United States, Canada—and yes, even in civilized England. In fact, I have seen cannibalism everywhere I have seen human culture. Indeed, right now on the planet there are things going on that make Fijian cannibalism look like a family barbecue.

I have seen cannibalism everywhere I have seen human culture.

Cannibalism: human beings, consuming and being consumed by their fellow human beings. Like those first missionaries to Fiji, I am "most deeply impressed" by the savage and inhuman atrocities that are practiced "as a matter of course"—not just within a stone's throw of my own home but better yet, beamed right into my living room. Daily I see the bodies of men, women and children "cut up with as much *sang-froid* as a butcher displays in dismembering an ox". I watch "the gods" get their share and the rest distributed among the men, and I notice that if the supply is large enough, women and children get a share.

Tastes differ, but to many human flesh is a "delicacy". I have seen the decks of battleships smeared with the blood of victims, slain "in the line of duty" to god and country. I have seen men "sacrificed" to give strength to the "posts" that support our institutional "structures"—and it is a mistake to think that we consume only our enemies taken in war....

Another custom which "harrows the feelings" is "the strangling of widows": the denial of rights to women, children and visible minorities who are least able to defend themselves. No less appalling is the manner in which the old and infirm are treated: "They are sometimes quickly given to understand (where it is needed) that they are a nuisance to their friends and relatives". I witness war-torn creatures plead for a cessation to the stomping and drought-stricken victims beg for a drink of water, but in such cases the community instinct operates with irresistible power.

Right now on the planet there are things going on that make Fijian cannibalism look like a family barbecue.

Then there are those who, in the course of their personal or professional endeavours, get "bitten by a shark". Their "friends and relatives" are quick to exchange views on the subject: the poor victims are often "strangled the same night".

"For such incredulity has been forced to yield to indisputable and repeated evidence" of which *any* culture can supply enough to convince a universe, "that man can fall so low as *habitually* to feed upon his fellow-men".

I shall cite well authenticated instances of such "horrors" in the hope that their narration will be far more profitable than revolting.

THE SECRET INGREDIENT

There are some who still do not believe cannibalism was a part of *any* culture at *any* time. It's a myth, they say, perpetrated by anthropologists—because in all our travels to strange and faraway places, none of us has actually *seen* any of these so-called savage people consuming one another. Instead, say our detractors, we confuse fact for fiction when we take for real, stories recorded in the logs of the trading ships and the journals of the missionaries. In other words, we anthropologists suffer from a curious case of "cultural literacy": we know it, even when we don't see it.

Well, this "Cookbook" not only reveals how people used to eat each other in the past, it also contains thirty "Recipes" describing cannibalism that is going on today—not just "over there", among savage people who have all kinds of strange customs anyway, but right here at home in our so-called civilized societies. There are plenty of people performing the rituals and plenty more willing to be their victims.

Why do they do it? In most cases people are not even aware they are doing it. The reason is because they suffer from a curious case of "cultural **ill**iteracy". Unlike the anthropologists who *know it even when they don't see it*, these people *don't know it even when they **do** see it*.

And what of their victims? Add to their cultural illiteracy a case of cultural blindness as well. Not only do they not know it: they can be looking right at it and not even see it. Fish don't see water. Birds don't see air. People don't see culture—not their own, anyway. We follow the dictates of our social systems much as we respond to post-hypnotic suggestion. Robots we are, poised and willing to do and to be all manner of human sacrifice.

We follow the dictates of our social systems much as we respond to post-hypnotic suggestion.

What do we do to stop being robots? It is not that there is something to be *done;* there is something to be *seen.* And that something requires not only that we know the "language" of culture but that we are also able to read between the lines! It is a tricky thing to do because when it comes to reading culture, most people are *spellbound.*

Some refer to this spellbound state as "false consciousness". By "false consciousness" they do not mean that we are in error in either an intellectual or ethical sense: it's not about being wrong or being bad. Rather, it is consciousness that is false in the sense of being based on *illusion.* It is about not being able to see through something, or not seeing something for what it really is.

Fish don't see water. Birds don't see air. People don't see culture—not their own, anyway.

Culture acts on us in much the same way as does a magician with his magic tricks. Through the simple yet subtle art of misdirection, the magician holds an entire audience in his power. If they were to "shift the direction of their look" and see his sleight of hand, they could release themselves from the spell. But they don't know where to look—and at a deeper psychological level, they don't *want* to! They don't want the spell to be broken. They want to be fooled—and they are willing to pay the price. They have literally bought into the illusion. So the magician does what he does best: he allows people to deceive themselves.

It is the same with culture. We don't know where to look—and at a deeper psychological level, we don't want to! We don't want the spell to be broken and we are willing to pay the price for buying into the illusion.

It's not that there is something to be done; there is something to be seen.

"False consciousness": the great cultural spell, the secret ingredient in cannibal cookery. While it is our *fate* as *social* beings, it need not be our *destiny* as *human* beings.

A SHORT GUIDE TO CULINARY TERMS

Once during a visit to New Zealand, I lodged at a guest house in the town of Rotorua on the north island. The establishment was operated by an older, though not elderly, couple. After check-in, the lady of the house accompanied me to my room and made things comfortable for me. As she left, she turned in the doorway and asked, "Would you like my husband to come and knock you up in the morning?"

I had heard that New Zealanders were very friendly....

"Oh, no thank-you." I think I sounded casual but I was shocked out of my complacency. (For readers from New Zealand—and civilized England—being "knocked up", in North American vernacular, is an awakening of a different sort for a woman of child-bearing years, which I was.)

We are immediately on guard when language is put to different usage in another culture—but we fail even to notice when it is distorted in our own. Why? Because of the cultural spell.

"Spell" is a very tricky word. As a noun it refers to a strong compelling influence or attraction. A spell is a charm, an incantation, a spoken set of words believed to have magical power. "Spell" is also a verb; to spell is to bewitch, to signify.

"Spell" also means to form words with letters, symbols or signs. We give all these different meanings to one simple word—and in cannibal cookery, "spell" is *all* of these things. That's because culture *is* a spell; through the charm of language, we are bound when we think we are free.

Here's how it is "spelled out". In linguistics, the smallest unit of sound that carries a meaning is called a morpheme (think "morphine"). Some morphemes are free and some are bound: free when they can stand on their own, bound when they are tied to another sound.

Culture is a spell; through the charm of language, we are bound when we think we are free.

Take, for example, the free morpheme *ease,* which refers to freedom from physical discomfort or mental agitation. The body is miraculously designed as a vehicle for taking the human journey. When we disturb its equilibrium, notice how it responds with a cold or a fever to cleanse itself of toxins, how a headache or acid indigestion is a natural attempt by the body to restore its state of ease.

Add the bound morpheme *dis-* to *ease* and we get a new word with an entirely different meaning. *Disease* refers to a disordered or unwholesome condition and results when the body's self-healing mechanism can no longer handle the physical and mental stresses battering its equilibrium.

Consider how one can be passed off as the other—how we have been conditioned to believe that the body's self-healing mechanism is the *disease,* and the symptoms are to be eliminated by quick and easy chemical remedies! The advertising language (think "languish") says it all. There's "extra strength", it's "recommended by Dr. Mom", and "Oh, what a relief it is!" In the process of treating as disease the body's attempt to restore equilibrium, we create *real* disease—and then we come to believe that "disease" is normal! Disease in place of ease; bound in place of free.

Now consider the free morpheme *garb* which means "to clothe, dress, array". Look around the planet and notice how it is garbed, how nature is magnificently arrayed: the lustrous furs of animals, the breathing foliage of trees, the protective skins of fruits and vegetables.... Have you ever noticed how the skin of every banana fits perfectly, and how oranges come in little sections wrapped in gourmet packaging. (That's one thing you can say for God: She sure can cook!)

Look again and notice where *garb* has been turned into *garbage:* where the furs of animals are draped over models to promote the fashion industry; where trees are pressed into newsprint to bolster the advertising industry; where oils are refined into packaging to promote the fast-food industry.... Dead animals, clear-cut forests, holes in the ozone, PCB's, dioxins, heptachlors.... *Garb* turned into *garbage.*

Or take this one: *entity,* which means existence as opposed to nonexistence. Add a little Freudian "id"—the "pleasure principle"—and what do you have? *Identity:* five billion little creatures out there—not revelling in the joy of their existence or contemplating the mystery of life—but scrambling about trying to "be somebody", as though identity were existence. Again, we are bound when we think we are free.

The idea is to "shift the direction of the look"...so that we might break the cultural spell.

Each of the thirty "Recipes" in the Cannibal's Cookbook is built on a pair of "culinary" terms. The first word, in most cases a free morpheme, refers to a condition in nature and reflects a state of "raw" innocence, of possibility, of purity. The second word is a bound form of the first, reflecting a "cooked" or *cultured* counterpart, a process which alters or distorts that natural state or potential.

The raw and the cooked: like *ease/disease, garb/garbage, entity/ identity,* these pairs of culinary terms have a singular purpose—to shock us out of our complacency. The idea is to "shift the direction of the look", as it were, so that we might realize how we are bound when we think we are free; so that we might know the difference between saying what we mean and meaning what we say; in short, so that we might break the cultural spell.

PART II

RECIPES FOR HUMAN SACRIFICE

Recipe # 1
PRESSING THEM DOWN

From **AUTHOR**
(the creator of
something)
To **AUTHORITY**
(the power to
command)

I'm in a small village on an outer island in Fiji. A woman has just died—the first death to occur in the village since I began my anthropological research here six weeks ago. I know life cycle rituals—birth, marriage, death—reveal a lot about a culture so I want to observe carefully the activities surrounding this event, but I don't know exactly where to position myself to get the bird's eye view.

I instruct Tau, my young Fijian research assistant, to "walk me through it", as it were, to put me in the right place at the right time. Then next time I'll know where to go and what to look for myself.

Tau takes me to the dead woman's house. It's a small building made of wood, suspended on concrete blocks. It now becomes the *vale ni mate,* the "house of death". Inside, women from the village prepare the body and lay it on top of a pile of new mats. The men gather in a temporary shelter made of palm fronds, which is affixed to one side of the house. There they mix the ceremonial kava drink.

Delegations of kin and friends arrive. The visiting men make presentations of whales' teeth, and drink kava. The women sit with the body inside where the formal mourning takes place. With each arrival, the women in the delegation suddenly break into mournful cries, and after a suitable period of time, the crying just as suddenly stops. Another delegation arrives. And it happens again—and again. It's a "group-mind" ritual: they begin and end their wailing on cue.

I stay with the women in the death house. After a few hours, a young girl leans into the doorway. *"Mai kana,"* she whispers to me, "Come and eat". I follow her to the chief's hut where women from the clan are dishing out huge quantities of beef, pork, fish, taro, yams and cassava. They serve us according to rank: chiefs and men first, women and children last. I am served with the men; I'm still a guest—and I'm white.

It's a "group-mind" ritual: they begin and end their wailing on cue.

After the feasting, we move to the church for the funeral service, and then to a prepared grave a short distance from the village. There is no cemetery as such. They wrap the body in new mats and lower it into the grave. Family and kin take turns sprinkling dirt on the mats. Then people quietly leave the burial site and return to the village.

That's that—or so I think.

Back in the village Tau seeks me out and escorts me once again to the "house of death". Inside, on the wooden floor covered by a single layer of pandanus mats, are several older women from the village—women whose child-bearing and child-tending duties are for the most part finished. There are about ten of them and they are lying in a huddle in the middle of the floor. It's quite a sight. They are without exception what one might politely describe as "full-figured", after years of consuming large quantities of starchy root crops—often the only food left by the time they get to eat.

I remain in this house with these "full-figured" grannies who just lie on the floor. They chat a bit, but for the most part they just lie there. I wait—and I wait. Nothing happens. After about five hours someone comes to get us and takes us to the chief's hut for dinner.

That's that—or, again, so I think—because after dinner, as they prepare to leave, the grannies beckon me to come with them again. We return to the "house of death" where they take up their same positions on the floor. I should tell you that this floor is very hard and the mat is very thin; it's extremely uncomfortable—but they keep lying there. I sit off to one side near the doorway watching them lie there doing nothing!

Why on earth do they keep on doing something that doesn't get them anywhere!

A few hours pass. Tau pokes his head in the doorway and asks me how I'm doing. I tell him it hasn't started yet, that they're just lying here on the floor doing nothing. "That's what they're here to do," he says, "to lie on the floor." I ask him how long they're going to be doing this lying on the floor. He answers, "Four days."

"Four days! I'm out of here!"

By now I know better than to ask the question—but I ask it anyway. "Why are they doing this?" I get the same response I always get: "It's the custom."

The custom, it turns out, is called *bikabika* (pronounced *mbikambika*). Any more than that they can't seem to tell me. I look for the word in my Fijian dictionary. It's not there but I do see the word *bika*; it's a verb meaning "to press down". I have discovered that in the Fijian language, sometimes nouns are constructed by repeating the verb form, so *bikabika* could be translated as the "pressing down".

Over the next four days I peer in on the full-figured grannies from time to time. They are still lying there doing nothing—except for one minor change. They are now complaining of headache and backache, upset stomach and indigestion, constipation and insomnia. I wonder why! They ask me for "medicine". I have a mild painkiller which I give them—but they just keep on lying there, doing themselves in; so after a while, I won't give it to them anymore.

A few weeks later I am at the archives in Suva, the Fijian capital. I dig into the records of early Fijian practices concerning death. I find that in pre-contact Fiji—that is, before Methodist missionaries and British colonists had their way— Fijians buried their deceased inside their own thatch huts. They just took up the mats, dug a hole, interred the body, replaced the dirt, and spread the mats again—which left a hump in the middle of the floor. What better way to rectify this inconvenience than to engage the services of full-figured grannies who are otherwise free from familial duties. Presto! *Bikabika!* And this "pressing down" would take about four days.

Living members of the family can then get on with their living—and as time goes by, offspring marry and build a thatch hut of their own. The old family home—perfectly bio-degradable—decomposes and falls to the ground, revealing the eternal resting place of the long-deceased parents. No cemetery is necessary. Brilliant!

They just took up the mats, dug a hole, interred the body, replaced the dirt, and spread the mats again.

The Fijians originated *bikabika* in response to a natural human need. They were the authors of their own lives. However, when they lost sight of the purpose because of some-one else's agenda, the very thing they originated ended up controlling them. In short, *author* became *authority*, and *bikabika* started pressing down the living rather than the dead.

Why can't they see this! Why on earth do they keep on

doing something that doesn't get them anywhere! Especially when, in the process, they end up with headaches and back-aches, upset stomachs and indigestion, constipation and insomnia. They must be crazy!

Then it hits home to me—literally—because I realize I've seen this before. I've seen it on commuter trains and crowded buses, in rush hour traffic jams and on sprawling freeways, in spiralling office towers and crowded tenement buildings, on stretches of commercial farmland and in choking facto-ries, in all manner of schools and training institutions: hu-man beings, pressed down by someone else's agenda, per-forming meaningless tasks in uncomfortable positions.

And at the end of the day, what do they see for their efforts? The CBS/CBC/NBC/BBC/ABC/NFK/CNN evening news, a fragmented record of their cultural ails, interrupted at calculated intervals with messages promising fast relief from headache and backache, upset stomach and indiges-tion, constipation and insomnia: drugs to numb the body and the mind so they will offer themselves up to be pressed down yet another day.

Bikabika!

"Whatever may have been the origin of man-eating in Fiji—whether famine or supersti-tion—there is not the slightest cause for its continuance. Food of every kind abounds.... The land gives large supply spontaneously, and, undoubtedly, is capable of supporting a hundred times the number of its present inhabitants."

—Rev. Thomas Williams

BREAKING THEM

From MASS
(the breaking of bread
in spiritual union)

To MASSACRE
(indiscriminate killing)

One of the last things my father did was bake bread. It was a favourite recipe of his, with molasses and oatmeal. He intended to eat it, of course; he didn't know he was going to die that night. For his funeral, his only remaining brother flies across the continent from Nova Scotia on Canada's east coast to British Columbia on the west and, as a symbolic gesture, my mother gives him Dad's last loaf of bread to take home. My uncle says he will bring together all the relatives there for "the breaking of the bread" in memory of my father. It is very fitting, because my uncle still lives on the homestead where my father was born.

He intended to eat it, of course; he didn't
know he was going to die that night.

Back home, my uncle carefully wraps and refrigerates the bread to preserve it for the commemoration. A day or two later, while driving along the highway, he picks up a hitch-hiker who turns out to be an interesting sort of hippie heading nowhere in particular. So my uncle takes the stranger home with him and, in typical Maritime fashion, invites the young man to find himself something to eat while he (my uncle) tends to chores in the field. When he returns to the house a while later, my dear father's brother discovers the hippie has consumed the entire loaf of bread.

My father's "last supper": bread, taken and eaten in complete love and acceptance, by someone who is rather mysteriously "called to his table".

Relatives at both ends of the continent are aghast! Of all the things that stranger could have taken and eaten from the refrigerator, why did it have to be my father's last loaf of bread!

I think it's wonderful. It's the perfect communion. My father's "last supper": bread, taken and eaten in complete love and acceptance, by someone who is rather mysteriously "called to his table". It is the quintessence of the Christian mass, replicated on that *first* last supper by those who were just as mysteriously called. My father would have understood that. It was an act based on pure spirit, the spirit which gives life to Christianity in its nascent form: in fact, the same spirit that speaks through all major world religions in their original design.

As bread was broken through the centuries, however, something seems to have been forgotten. Perhaps it was because of the ritual itself: the paraphernalia, the rites, the robes, the dogma, the liturgy, the symbols.... Human spirit got *converted* into psychic energy, then *diverted* to the task of perpetuating the ritual, then the institution, then the empire.... Christianity became Christendom. The feast turned bitter. Mass turned to massacre. There is nothing bloodier than a holy war.

History bears it out. Crusades, holy wars, holy empires—all defended in the name of the one who offered bread to those who came to his table. The stranger who needed to be fed was savagely and indiscriminately killed. Today, numerous ongoing bloody conflicts are still based on religion and ideology as though a grotesque and greedy god were demanding human sacrifice.

He took bread and broke it.... And he said, "Take and eat.... Do this in remembrance of me...."

Christianity became Christendom. The feast turned bitter. Mass turned to massacre. There is nothing bloodier than a holy war.

Cannibals for Christ! We have forgotten to break bread, not people.

"On reaching the middle of the town, the body was thrown down before the Chief, who directed the priest to offer it in due form to the war-god. Fire had been placed in the great oven, and the smoke rose above the old temple, as the body was again drawn to the shore to be cut up."

—Rev. Thomas Williams

Recipe # 3
WRINGING THEIR NECKS

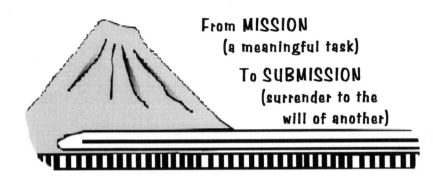

From MISSION
(a meaningful task)

To SUBMISSION
(surrender to the
will of another)

Much of my childhood is spent as part of a family logrolling act travelling the Sports Show circuits in the United States and Canada. During these years I meet and work with many talented people, all of them polished performers in their athletic and artistic fields.

One encounter sticks in my memory: I am 12 years old and we are in Chicago. Three young men from Japan do the closing act in the show this year—which is unusual because they are not even performers. They have been brought here from the city of Gifu in central Honshu, the main island of Japan, to demonstrate the unusual Japanese art of cormorant fishing.

What they do is put ties around the necks of the cormorants and attach a leash. Then from the deck of their boat, the three "fishermen" send the birds into the water. The hungry cormorants dive and catch fish, but because of the ties around their necks they are unable to swallow their catch. The men pull the birds from the water and with their bare hands squeeze the fish from the throats of the cormorants. Then they send them into the water again. Because the birds are still hungry they each go after another fish, and another, and another.... The routine is repeated until the fishermen have their quota. At the end of the process these unusual "sportsmen" give the very hungry cormorants a small portion of the take. The birds get to swallow this time; it is enough to keep them alive and entice them to go through the exercise yet another day.

At the time, I am more interested in culture than I am in fishing. My new acquaintances, who barely speak English, oblige my curiosity by teaching me words and phrases in Japanese. *"Mushi mushi, adegato,"* ("Hello, thank-you,") I repeat after them; *"Ichi, ni, san, shi, go."* ("One, two, three, four, five.") Simple things like that. Before we say *sayanara* in Chicago, they instruct me in a phrase with which I am to greet them when we meet again at the Los Angeles Sports Show in a few weeks.

"Anata wawata kushi o suki desuka"—is the way I remember it. I recite it with energy and affection when I meet them in the City of Angels. They chuckle with delight— so I say it every time I see them. They never do tell me what it means. It is a very long time before I find out to my embarrassment that I was repeatedly asking these three guys, "Do you love me?"

Years later a Canadian-Japanese joint project takes me to the land of the cormorant fishermen. I am stationed in Kobe, not far from Gifu, from where I commute by train to near and far locations within the country: Kyoto, Himeji, Hiroshima, Tokyo....

No matter what time of day or night I travel, I see them: Japanese businessmen propped there in their seats, dressed in suits with ties around their necks, dozing and sleeping as they commute to and from their various work destinations.

Those who are not asleep look like they should be. Without exception, it seems to me, these breadwinners are exhausted. They even give me a new word for my Japanese vocabulary: *karoshi.* It means "death from overwork".

Why do they do it? To cash in on the booming Japanese economy? To enjoy a high standard of living? Perhaps to become infinitely wealthy within the giant corporations? No. They are not cashing in, they are not enjoying a high standard of living, and they are not becoming infinitely wealthy. The truth is they are forced to rent themselves out in order to survive while the booming Japanese economy keeps inflating their hard-earned yen. It costs $75 (U.S.) just to buy a cantaloupe! And at the end of an arduous work day that stretches into the night, they return to their families in tiny rented quarters. Most Japanese workers cannot even afford to buy a home.

They even give me a new word for my Japanese vocabulary:* karoshi. *It means "death from overwork".

They are just like those cormorants— attached to the leashes of the giant corporations who put ties around their necks. They "fish" but they do not get to keep the catch. At the end of the process they are allotted a small portion of the take—enough to keep them alive and to entice them to go through the exercise yet another day.

And it's not just in Japan. The alarming thing about Japan is that we hold it up as a model! The truth is that corporations everywhere thrive on and profit from the extraction of vital human energy. They roam the world at will, unhindered by national boundaries while people, locked within borders, must bid with their vital energy for the privilege of serving them.

In the future, giant corporations will have even more control over our lives. They will determine where we live and how far we move, what tasks we perform and how we perform them, what schedules we keep and what we do with our time. They will have more influence over our lives than any other single entity—and they are accountable to no one!

When we lose control of our lives, we lose sight of our *mission*. Where there is no mission people fall prey to *submission*—like cormorants, attached to leashes with ties around their necks, expecting no more than a paycheque at the end of the day.

In the future, giant corporations...will have more influence over our lives than any other single entity—and they are accountable to no one!

Submission: about as far removed from a course in intellectual self-defence as walking up to the guys who tie the necks and unwittingly reciting, "Do you love me?"

"A Chief has been known to kill several men for rollers, to facilitate the launching of his canoes, the 'rollers' being afterwards cooked and eaten."

—Rev. Thomas Williams

Recipe # 4
GOING FOR THE JUGULAR

From SERVE
(to meet a need)

To SERVITUDE
(submission to a master)

I'm in Nepal, marvelling at the scenery and breathing the fresh mountain air. All about me is an uninterrupted display of natural magnificence. Here one can almost feel a respite from the constraints of the social world.

All about me is an uninterrupted display of natural magnificence.

Perhaps that is why the following incident strikes me so profoundly. It unfolds at a temple compound in Katmandu. I notice a small crowd gathered in one section of the courtyard, staring at the upper chamber of the temple. There a young girl is smiling at them through an ornately-carved open window. We are told she is the *Kumari Devi*, a manifestation of the ten-armed goddess *Durga*. Chosen at the age of four, she has been incarcerated on the upper floor of this 16th century temple, her feet not permitted to touch the ground. An older woman stands beside her, watching carefully. Someone in the crowd prepares to take the young girl's picture.

The older woman waves her arms in protest: the *Kumari Devi* is not to be photographed....

The young girl, we learn, has not yet reached *menarche*. In other words, she has not yet started to bleed. That qualifies her as a powerful symbol of both purity and fertility: purity, because blood is a highly polluting substance in Hindu ideology; fertility, because she represents the potential of future life.

The prepubescent girl spends precious years of her young life tucked away in the upper chamber of the temple attended by an older woman. But the attendant, it turns out, is more a master than a servant—she only appears to protect the girl. In reality, she is there to safeguard the purity and fertility of the society at large. That's why she shields the *Kumari Devi* from the photographer. Nothing must be allowed to compromise her symbolic potency.

What will happen when the young girl starts to bleed? Simple: they will let her go and find someone else to take her place—but they will keep the attendant.

Bizarre.

Here is a society indulging in a form of "wealth" extraction by consuming the very lifeblood of one of its own, using another as an accomplice. And when the "victim" no longer has blood to give to the enterprise, the accomplice will stand idly by as she is replaced by someone else.

What will happen when the young girl starts to bleed? Simple: they will let her go, and find someone else to take her place.

Well, at first it feels bizarre—but the longer I stand here and gaze up at this scene, the more it starts to feel familiar. Where have I seen this before? Where else have I witnessed something or somebody pretending to protect but in reality allowing "wealth" to be extracted from the very lifeblood of people who are then passed over once they no longer have blood left for the enterprise?

In government, that's where. Governments appear to act on behalf of the people but in reality they safeguard the interests of the elite. Human history bears this out. There are roughly four stages through which societies have evolved: an initial stage of hunter-gatherers, a second stage of subsistence agriculture, a third stage of feudal ownership, and a final stage of capitalism (socialist and communist systems aside).

Governments appear to act on behalf of the people but in reality they safeguard the interests of the elite.

Each of these stages is accompanied by institutions suited to its needs. In the first stage there is no "private property" as such, so there are no institutional safeguards for it. With the advent of agriculture comes private property, and as society moves to feudalism and capitalism, protective institutions fortified by law and order gain increasing strength and prominence.

The institutions of private property are not for the protection of people. "Civil government," wrote Adam Smith in *The Wealth of Nations,* ". . . is in reality instituted for the defense of the rich against the poor, or of those who have some property against those who have none at all." *Laissez-faire* capitalism, as he envisaged it, was to become the system of perfect liberty—but government stood in the way by catering to special-interest groups, thus preventing the competitive system from having its "benign effect".

Smith's notion of "natural liberty" was founded on a "free market" that served the best interests of all—but it could not be put into practice if government were under the influence of "the mean rapacity, the monopolizing spirit of merchants and manufacturers, who neither are, nor ought to be, the rulers of mankind".*

If Smith, the much-touted spiritual guru of free enterprise, were alive today he would be aghast at the level of monopoly control. Modern governments sanction wealth extraction more than ever before: such as Canada did by selling—yes, *selling*—the Nechako River in north-central British Columbia to Alcan Aluminum for its private commercial use, with the resulting devastation of the fish population and live-lihood of indigenous people; such as the signing of the North American Free Trade Agreement, which allows trans-national corporations to benefit from low wages, low environmental standards, and low corporate taxes while workers face in-creasing competition for declining reward; such as income tax systems that allow corporations to contribute little or no taxes while wage-earners are burdened with paying for ever-increasing national debts.

Governments, which should function to *serve* the people, instead put the people in *servitude* with the result that the worker in society, as in the days of Adam Smith, "generally becomes," to use his words, "as stupid and ignorant as it is possible for a human being to become."

I certainly do not mean to suggest that workers in soci-ety are inherently stupid or ignorant. It is simply that they have put their trust in an attendant who, it turns out, is more a *master* than a *servant*—a master who will sit idly by when they are replaced because they no longer have blood to give to the enterprise.

"A woman taken from a town besieged by Ra Undreundre... was placed in a large wooden dish and cut up alive, that none of the blood might be lost."
— Rev. Thomas Williams

Recipe # 5
MAKING A KILLING

From ART
(creating beautiful
things)
To ARTIFICE
(subtle deception)

Papeete, December, 1988. Almost a hundred years after the great French post-impressionist painter, Paul Gauguin, arrived in Tahiti.

"A governor, a police officer, and a dealer in tobacco and postage stamps. Already here!" he had exclaimed. "My God!! It is Europe, the Europe I thought I had finished with, in a form even worse, with colonial snobbery and the heaping of our customs, fashions, vices and crazes in a manner so grotesque that it borders on caricature." It had taken the French only a few short decades to turn this little whaling harbour into a pretentious colonial outpost.

A century after Gauguin's arrival, the colonists are still here. Papeete abounds with evidence of the ongoing "French connection": the residence of the High Commissioner, the Territorial Assembly, the post office...governors, police officers and dealers in postage stamps! Add to this mix the tourist bureau, banks, bars and restaurants. Papeete is growing, in no small part because of France's nuclear testing program.

I am staying at the *Royal Papeete*, located in the heart of the city. It is situated on Boulevard Pomare, the main thoroughfare stretching alongside the waterfront. It must have been a fine hotel in its day and still has a strange sense of grandeur about it. I like the old feel to it, the aged wood panelling and the worn carpets—something the newer resort hotels lack altogether.

A century after Gauguin's arrival, the colonists are still here. Papeete abounds with evidence of the ongoing "French connection".

I have come to Tahiti to trace the path of Gauguin in his search for "a savage alternative" to his own culture. He stayed only a few months in Papeete. Disillusioned with the Tahitian capital, he went up the coast to Pacca where he settled by the sea. A few months later, he moved further along the coast to Mataiea where there were only natives around him. There he could think and paint, and there a native girl came to share his hut with him. With young Teha'amana he spent his happiest time in Tahiti.

Today, it's a beautiful drive along the coast but there is little evidence of "the savage alternative" even when one gets outside the urban centre. I find the spots where the painter lived, and then make my way to the Gauguin Museum situated in a lovely garden just past Mataiea. It tells the story of the artist with "the savage dream", but few of his works are here. Instead, there is a map of the world showing where the masterpieces are currently located: London, Paris, New York, Boston, Geneva, Munich, Copenhagen, Bern, Moscow, Leningrad...a lot of them are in Leningrad.

Gauguin: one of those French artists who struggled and succeeded in the attempt to revolutionize art in the last century. At that time, admission to the French art community was controlled by "the Academy", and artists with anything but a conventional, Classical approach were generally refused entry. Today their works are more cherished than the scores of academic paintings they once challenged. Corbet, Millet, Manet, Renoir, Monet—the Realists and the Impressionists who rebelled against antiquated dogma and artistic tradition; these were the artists whose subject matter was the world of nature, and they conveyed their personal immediate perception of it. Their work has a ring of truth to it, a look of authenticity, a feeling of something experienced, understood and carefully recorded.

In his Tahitian search for the primitive life and the source of human culture, Gauguin came to believe that painting should express inner emotions and ideas. From this point in his career the life of the mind and the soul would take precedence over the senses. He rejected external appearances. The *subject*, he felt, must be sought "not in the world the eye can see, but in the mysterious centre of thought".

"I feel that in my art I am right," stated Gauguin after he had been in Polynesia for some time, "but will I have the strength to express this convincingly enough? In any case, I shall have done my duty, and even if my work does not endure, there will always remain the memory of an artist who freed painting from many of its old academic failings...."*

The subject, he felt, must be sought "not in the world the eye can see, but in the mysterious centre of thought".

Gauguin's art has endured. Today his canvases are priceless masterpieces, not only because of their exotic subject matter, or the way he dared to violate existing conventions and academic taboos, but also because they satisfy the purpose of great art. Gauguin awakens something deep within us, that which is "in the mysterious centre of thought"—spirit. That spirit is somehow present all along, but only realized at a higher state of consciousness. Gauguin, like thinkers and painters before and after him, went in search of it. Not that he ever found it: it was too illusive for that, and seemed always just beyond his grasp. Yet the artist in him *intuited* it and somehow the quest kept him going.

"Today I have hit rock bottom," he wrote during his sojourn in Tahiti. "Beaten by poverty and, worst of all, this illness that has brought me to an altogether too early old age. I do not think it will give me any respite to finish my work.... I will make a last effort next month to go to live at Fatu Hiva, the one Marquesan island where there is still some cannibalism. I hope that there in that altogether wild element, that complete solitude will give me a last burst of enthusiasm which will rejuvenate my imagination and lead to the fulfillment of my talent before I die."

Gauguin did go to Fatu Hiva, and there, broken by poverty and ill-health, he died. "Out of my window," he wrote from his deathbed,

> everything is growing dark. The dances are ended, the soft melodies have died away; but it is not still. In a crescendo the wind rushes through the branches: the great dance begins. The cyclone is in full swing, the river overflows. Everything is in flight: rocks, trees, corpses carried down to the sea.... Then the sun returns, the lofty coconut trees lift up their plumes again. Man does likewise. The great anguish is over; joy has returned. The sea smiles like a child, the reality of yesterday becomes a fable. And one forgets it.

Gauguin was brought to a premature death because those who might have nurtured his life and his creativity were blinded by antiquated dogma and artistic tradition. By their studied neglect, they were "making a killing".

A few months later I'm back in Canada, at the National Art Gallery in Ottawa. The gallery is an impressive piece of art in its own right with a spectacular main viewing hall to champion its "masterpiece". And what is displayed in this prominent space? A Gauguin? A Renoir or Monet? Or a major work by one of the Canadian Group of Seven?

No. A huge canvas by an American artist consisting of three solid vertical stripes: blue, red, blue. That's it! So annoyed are local residents at this "art" that they are painting perfect duplicates of this "strip of stripes" to display in their front yards. It is a form of protest, for what else can they do! While Canadian artists struggle against antiquated dogma and artistic tradition, the National Art Gallery of Canada sinks a whopping $1.8 million of their tax money into this artifice!

("My God!! It is Europe, the Europe I thought I had finished with, in a form even worse, with colonial snobbery and the heaping of our customs, fashions, vices and crazes in a manner so grotesque that it borders on caricature.")

Someone is making a killing—while the Gauguins of this world struggle to survive.

"Cannibalism among this people is one of their institutions; it is interwoven in the elements of society, and it is regarded by the mass as a refinement."

— Rev. Thomas Williams

Recipe # 6

GETTING UNDER THEIR SKIN

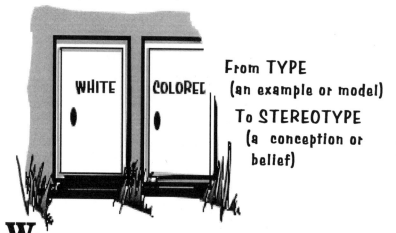

From TYPE
(an example or model)

To STEREOTYPE
(a conception or belief)

When I was very young, the life and work of my family took us to the deep south of the United States. It used to strike me as odd that black people sat at the backs of buses and in the balconies of churches—but everybody seemed to go along with it, and I was only a kid so what did I know?

On one occasion when I was six years old we were travelling by car through Alabama and we stopped at a gas station. I had to go to the bathroom so my mother told my older sister to take me. As we made our way, I noticed there were two ladies' washrooms, one labelled "White", the other "Colored". My sister headed toward the "White" one. I said, "Let's go to the coloured one." She said, "Why would you want to go to the coloured one?" I replied, "Why go to a plain white washroom when you can go to one that's coloured!"

She stopped short in her tracks and gave me one of those "older sister" looks. "Don't be so stupid," she exclaimed. "That washroom is not coloured. It's for coloured people!"

I hadn't even thought of that! I was so naive. Thank God! My sister had it right—but I think she was wrong. I didn't tell her so at the time. She was a lot bigger than me.

Forty years later, I still haven't told her. I mean, it is

such a blatant form of prejudice. Yet if you ask most people if they are prejudiced, they will probably say "no"—except perhaps white extremists like members of the Ku Klux Klan—and we feel repulsed by what they say and do. Maybe it's because they mirror something we don't want to look at in ourselves, something that is repressed.

"Why go to a plain white washroom when you can go to one that's coloured!"

The thing about repressed material is that it comes out in other ways, like slips of the tongue, forgetfulness, humour— especially humour. For example, something gets repressed in the American psyche after the Space Shuttle disaster and guess what: Challenger jokes appear! You've probably heard some, like, "Why did the astronauts not take a bath before lift-off?" Answer: "Because they knew they'd wash up on the coast of Florida later in the day." It's morbid, I know, but it relieves tension.

A lot of these jokes have to do with the school teacher on board. It is more traumatic somehow for a civilian to be killed because the others are military people, and the thing about military people is that we pay them to "do the dying" for us. Have you heard this one? "What's the big deal about the school ma'rm on the Shuttle: it's not the first time a teacher blew up in front of her class!" An experience too traumatic to deal with at face value becomes trivialized.

In Canada we have ethnic jokes about the people of New-foundland, the province with the lowest per capita income and the highest rates of unemployment. We call them "Newfie" jokes. Did you hear the one about the Newfie who dies and wants to be buried at sea? Six men drown digging his grave.

That's funny?

The joke presupposes that the people of Newfoundland haven't quite got "the smarts". It's instructive to look at the derivation of some of these "pre-judgments". For example, in an I.Q. test back in the fifties children in Newfoundland scored consistently lower than children in other parts of Canada. Why? Maybe it had something to do with the fact that there was a series of questions on the test relating to and based on oranges. At the time, there were no oranges being imported into Newfoundland!

Similar prejudgments are attributed to dark-skinned people in the United States. Here's a common type of joke. Adam and Eve are sitting around in the Garden of Eden and, probably because there is nothing better to do, they muse about whether they are black or white. Not able to ascertain it on their own, Eve suggests that Adam go up the mountain and ask God—which he does. When he comes back he says to Eve, "We are white." Eve says, "Is that what God told you?" Adam replies, "Well, he didn't just come out and say 'You are white.' He said 'You are that you are'." And Eve says, "Well, how on earth does that mean we are white?" to which Adam replies, "Well if we were black, He would have said 'You *is* that you *is*'."

My brother told me that one. He used to tell me racial jokes because I had such a reaction to them. Since I've been teaching Anthropology, I've paid more attention—so he keeps telling them to me but now he calls it "research".

That "I am" joke—you'll recall that God tells Moses his name is "I am that I am"—refers not to racial inferiority but to racial inequality. That's why we joke about it. It releases tension because we know damn well Afro-Americans don't get a fair shake. We put them where they are—and keep them there. Jokes literally spell it out.

If it isn't skin colour, we find some other basis for discrimination, such as age or sex— even the slant of the eyes!

Take this one, for example. It showed up at the time of school desegregation and forced busing in the United States. A white driver has a busload of black and white kids who, racially speaking, are fighting it out. He's fed up! He stops the bus, makes them all get out and gives them a hell of a lecture. "From now on," he says, "no more black and no more white. You're all...*green*. Do you get that? Green. Not black, not white, all green, okay? So now, no more fighting. Get back in the bus. Light green in the front, dark green in the back."

All of this is about prejudice. Easy to see because it's pretty negative stuff. We don't subscribe to it so we think we are not prejudiced.

There's another form of prejudice that doesn't show up quite so easily. It's hard even to recognize it as prejudice. It's the kind that encourages us to see others as different and separate from ourselves—and we are carefully taught it in school.

I got a good dose of it in Grade 5 Geography. We had this textbook called "Visits to Other Lands". There were stories about children from all over the world, illustrating how different they are from us. On the final exam, there was this question: "Of all the children, which would you most like to be, and why?" My sister got to Grade 5 ahead of me, of course, and she answered, "Olga from the fiords in Norway because of all the countries that is the one most like home." When I got the same question two years later I figured that must be the right answer because my sister had passed the course. However, by this time I was starting to think for myself and I answered, "Bunga from the jungles of Malaya because of all the countries that is the one most *unlike* home". I got a higher mark! Once again, my sister was "right" but I thought she was wrong. I didn't tell her, though, because she was still a lot bigger than me.

> **There's another form of prejudice that doesn't show up quite so easily...and we are carefully taught it in school.**

I grew up with these "different" ideas in my head and as a result, I developed a full-fledged "positive" prejudice. I went out of my way to be with people of other races and cultures. I preferred them, defended them, travelled great distances to live and work with them.... Just like my older sister, I was full of prejudice.

It's just human nature. Or is it? No. We are not prejudicial by *nature*. We are prejudicial by *culture*. We all grow up in culture. I grew up in the world of my sister. If she inherited a slightly different form of it, well, she was older than me—and the times, they were a-changin'!

So what does prejudice turn on? How do we get beyond it? It turns on our cultural conditioning. That's clear enough. Getting beyond it is trickier because it means getting beyond culture. Before you can get beyond culture, you've got to see *through* it—which is a matter of right education. Not the kind you get in school, mind you. That's training—and that's a large part of why we are so prejudiced in the first place.

Schooling teaches us to discriminate, to divide the whole into parts, to reduce things to categories. In other words, it conditions us to "pre-judge". Our cultural institutions perpetuate these "pre-judgments"—in short, "prejudices". They just carry us along. For example, it doesn't occur to a lot of people that it's downright unfriendly to have "coloreds" sitting at the backs of buses and in the balconies of churches. Why? Because they have been carefully conditioned to have it *not* occur to them.

Some years ago on American television—after the news about a thwarted peace march by "African" Americans in Alabama—I watch the NAACP image awards. That's a curious acronym, the "National Association for the Advancement of Colored People". At least "Black is Beautiful" has a bit of a ring to it. The problem is in stressing the *difference*, creating positive prejudice, perpetuating boundaries where none should exist.

Schooling teaches us to discriminate, to divide the whole into parts, to reduce things to categories.

If it isn't skin colour, we find some other basis for discrimination, such as age or sex—even the slant of the eyes! Where we don't have those "differences" to set boundaries, we can always look to more abstract categories like religion or nationality.

Black/white, dark green/light green.... The peculiar thing about a boundary is that it divides and separates, producing a myriad of problems. Rather than struggling to *solve* the problems created by the boundaries, wouldn't it make more sense to *dissolve* the boundaries that create the problems in the first place?

"If a Chief should not lower his mast within a day or two of his arrival at a place, some poor creature is killed and taken to him as 'the lowering of the mast.' In every case an enemy is preferred; but when this is impracticable, the first common man at hand is taken."

— Rev. Thomas Williams

Recipe # 7

CUTTING THEM DOWN TO SIZE

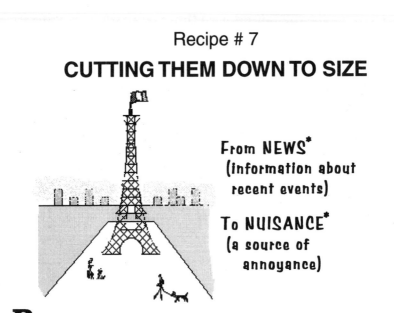

From NEWS*
(information about
recent events)

To NUISANCE*
(a source of
annoyance)

Paris, 1989. It's the French bicentennial. I'm staying at a small hotel across the street from UNESCO in the shadow of the Eiffel Tower. "CENT ANS", the 1889 centennial symbol spells out in bold lights along the still-impressive vertical steel structure. It's a double celebration for the French this year because it's also the two hundredth anniversary of the birth of a republican nation.

Think of it: an end to monarchy; the abolition of class privilege; a Declaration of Rights; suffrage by taxpayers—even if only a third of the population get to vote, and all of them are male. In one fell blow, it is the birth of liberty, equality and fraternity.

How did they do it? Was it perhaps because of the French philosophers who assumed leadership in the 18th century Enlightenment—men like Montesquieu with his views about limited government, or Voltaire and his interest in secular ethics and relativism, or possibly Rousseau with his notions about the inherent goodness of the human being? They represented a triumph of faith in human reason in the face of oppressive religious and political institutions.

But it is also the two hundredth anniversary of the bloody

Reign of Terror. The birth of republicanism in France un-
leashed a display of violence and brutality almost inconceiv-
able in light of its ideals. Unspeakable horrors were committed in the name of humanitarian principles while the crowds
cheered. If the storming of the Bastille signalled the birth of
a free nation, that same freedom was the child of a holo-
caust.

It's not that the French are different—as much as we or
they might like to think they are. The same enigmatic drama
that played itself out in this elegant capital two hundred years
ago epitomizes the contradictory world we all live in every
day. If there is anything that sets apart the current scene, it
is only that the stakes are higher now. The guillotine claimed
many, to be sure, but only one at a time. Now, we can take
out whole cities, whole nations, whole continents—and we
can still do it in the name of liberty, equality and fraternity!
Fundamentally we have not changed.

***It's not that the French are different—as much
as we or they might like to think they are.***

I check out of my hotel en route to Charles de Gaulle
airport. I pick up a French newspaper at the reception desk.
The headline this morning is from Beijing. It seems in the
dark of the night, the Chinese People's Army has moved in
and massacred students who were demonstrating for democratic reform in Tiananmen Square. A democratic revolution
crushed by a bloody reign of terror....

New information gave birth to the French Revolution:
news, pure and simple. It was a distortion of that same news
that allowed its deterioration into a reign of terror. News is
the cornerstone of freedom itself. Without the flow of new
information and ideas, there can exist no liberty, no equality, no fraternity/sorority.

How are we to get our news? From journalists, of course.
Journalists are the agents of the individual in the defence of
our liberty, equality and fraternity/sorority. They are the ones
who gather and analyze new information in order that we

citizens of the state can make enlightened decisions. The thought leaves me unsettled.

I look back at Paris as the British Airways jet climbs into the sky on its flight to London. Moments later a hostess hands me a copy of the *London Times*. There is a prominent picture of a young couple getting off an aircraft. The caption reads: "Charles and Diana arrive for vacation at Balmoral. A brisk wind greets Diana. Charles takes the wheel for the one-hour drive." How informative! This will certainly help the British make decisions in defense of their liberty and equality.

Reminds me of an item I once saw in the *Edmonton Journal* which is a fairly reputable Canadian newspaper. There was a picture of a plumpish woman descending the steps of an aircraft. She was wearing a flowery dress with matching hat and she was holding an umbrella. At the foot of the stairs a man in uniform was pointing to his head. Since he has no gun in his hand, we can rule out suicide. Caption? "Carrying her own umbrella, the Queen Mother arrived in Edmonton on Tuesday."

"Carrying her own umbrella." This will certainly help Canadians make enlightened decisions in defense of their liberty and equality!**

What is fascinating about these two stories is their apparent innocence, reflecting an almost-universal blind acceptance of institutionalized inequality.

How could Louis XVIth and his Austrian queen have indulged in such lavish opulence while the country was going bankrupt? How could the French aristocracy have enjoyed such tax privileges while heaping burdensome feudal obligations onto the peasants? How could the wife of Romanian dictator Ceausescu become the 14th richest woman in the world while her egalitarian communist countryfolk suffered in abject poverty? How can Queen Elizabeth the Second become one of the richest women in the world while the people of her "United Kingdom" face record unemployment, bankruptcies and housing repossessions?

It's not that journalists are *incapable* of seeing things as they are. It's that they are conditioned *not* to. That conditioning is strategically inculcated by those who have a vested interest in keeping things the way they are. Buckingham Palace is one big public relations front, spoon-feeding the media with "news" releases that perpetuate perks and privilege. Top-ranking news teams travel half way around the world to cover royal investitures and royal weddings. They willingly and compliantly flood the airwaves and journals with announcements of royal pregnancies and royal births, royal romances and royal weddings, royal breakups and royal makeups. They follow every move their royal highnesses make: getting off an airplane, driving in a car, falling off a horse, getting a piece of food caught in the throat.... Everything they do takes on a magnitude of import while their countryfolk struggle to have their basic democratic grievances addressed: unfair distribution of wealth, loss of meaningful work, inappropriate training and technology, lack of affordable housing, contaminated food, unsafe drinking water, polluted air....

It's not that journalists are **incapable** *of seeing things as they are. It's that they are* **conditioned** *not to.*

Journalists become unwitting accomplices in the same autocracy and inequality it is their duty to reveal. They forget the lesson of the French Revolution. They fail to recognize that "Her Royal Highness" means "our common lowness". They turn news into nuisance, relegating journalism to the role of affirming rather than questioning perks and privilege, thereby cutting people down to size.

"He first made a long, deep gash down the abdomen, and then cut all round the neck down to the bone, and rapidly twisted off the head from the axis. The several parts were then folded in leaves and placed in the oven."
— Rev. Thomas Williams

Recipe # 8
A CUT ABOVE THE REST

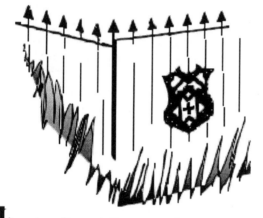

From GARB
(to clothe)

To GARBLE
(to misinterpret)

I'm standing at the gate of the Royal Tombs in Nuku'alofa in the tiny South Pacific island kingdom of Tonga. It's not a very lavish or even well-tended space considering it's the burial ground for Tonga's much respected and much admired royalty. The grounds are enclosed by a very plain and unattractive wire fence, and inside the enclosure the grass badly needs cutting. It seems an unfitting tribute to people of such rank and power.

Take "Queen" Salote, for example, whose long reign brought a period of unity and stability to Tonga. She was only 18 years old when she "became queen", and because she was a woman it was thought she wouldn't take part in Tongan politics. Wrong! In fact, she ran a very strong government with a clear sense of purpose and she did it with a dual goal in mind. First, she wanted to preserve the distinctive Tongan way of life; secondly, she wanted Tongans to be able to take advantage of what was best in the modern world.

To achieve these ends, Queen Salote set in motion a number of revolutionary changes. She formed the Tongan Traditions Committee and instituted festivals and national celebrations. She increased educational opportunities for young

Tongans. She sponsored health campaigns to attack the diseases of yaws, tuberculosis, typhoid fever and eye infections; she also started a school of nursing. She set up programs for clean water, population control, agricultural pest control, crop diversification, and the marketing of agricultural produce. She changed the system of land use and land distribution. She formed a Handicrafts Board which encouraged the sale of mats, basketry and tapa cloth to tourists. She increased the commercial shipping fleet to handle sales of copra (coconut meat) to overseas markets. She promoted the tourist industry to ease the country's reliance on copra. She invested surplus monies in a development fund which created a meteorological office, a telephone exchange, a new wharf, a tourist hotel and electrical system. She educated Tongans so that foreign experts would not be needed, and by the 1950's, the government was able to begin replacing offshore employees with trained Tongan nationals.

The list doesn't stop there. She brought about a number of other social changes as well. She gave women the vote, formed the Tongan Women's Progress Association to improve village conditions, set up the Tongan Red Cross and the Boy Scout and Girl Guide movements, started a radio station and a weekly newspaper....

I am telling you all this because before coming here to visit this remarkable woman's tomb, I watched on CBC television back in Canada another one of those British royal weddings—full of extravagant pomp and ceremony—for a "Duke and Duchess" who cannot claim to be even interested in any of the above. A guest commentator for the coverage remarked that during the coronation of Queen Elizabeth II, a certain Queen Salote from Tonga rode in an open carriage with her head uncovered to show deference to the British monarch. The reason that is significant is because it happened to be raining that day and Salote was the only distinguished guest who allowed herself to get wet. The anchor of Canada's public television network, flown to London especially for the occasion, responded, "I don't even know where Tonga is," to which the commentator replied, "Well, nobody did here either."

Well, gentlemen, Tonga is located north and a little east

of New Zealand, between latitudes 15 and 23.5 South and longitudes 173 and 177 West, just below the tropic of Capricorn and to the west of the international dateline. In fact, Tonga is the first place in the world to see the sun rise at the dawn of each new day—and they've seen a lot of them. Archaeologists have established that the islands of Tonga have been settled since at least 500 years before the birth of Jesus. From earliest times, the Tongans were controlled by chieftains, and their social organization was guided by four overriding principles: *mateaki* (loyalty), *fatongia* (obligation), *talangofua* (obedience), and *faka'apa'apa* (respect).

Tonga is the first place in the world to see the sun rise at the dawn of each new day— and they've seen a lot of them.

However, the exchange of the television commentators didn't end with geographical uncertainty. The Canadian anchor added, "She just arrived claiming she was the queen from there, did she?" It was a question that pointed to the absurdity of an island people pretending one among them is "royal", with all the perks and privileges of royalty. Of course, he was right—what a farce! What he didn't seem to realize is that he was visiting another island people pretending one among *them* was "royal", with all the perks and privileges of royalty. It's alright, it seems, for Britain—and by extension (or by colonial expansion) for Canada—to pretend it has a monarch. So blinded was he—and I suspect most of his television audience—that he didn't even realize the wizards of Buckingham Palace had just invented a family coat of arms for the commoner bride so they could pretend she was "royal", too; and that they "legitimized" the insignia by embroidering it onto her wedding dress! What a farce! Turning *garb* into *garble....*

The *Tui Tonga* (King of Tonga) was believed to be of divine origin, the son of the creator god *Tangaloa 'Eitumatupu'a*. He was a supreme and sacred ruler. (Sound like the divine right of kings?) "Whenever he walks out," wrote Captain Cook, observing the Tui Tonga in 1777, "all who meet him must sit down till he has passed. No person is suffered to be over his head; but on the contrary, all must come under his feet." Whenever he sat down, his attendants sat down in front of him, forming a semicircle. No-one was permitted to enter the area unless given permission by the *Tui Tonga*. Similarly, no person could pass near him or behind him—and it was, in Cook's words, "a glaring mark of rudeness" to speak to him while standing. Moreover, any house entered by the king immediately became taboo, and could never again be inhabited by its owner. Wrote Cook, "None of the most civilized nations have ever exceeded these islanders in the great order and regularity maintained on every occasion, in ready and submissive compliance with the commands of their chiefs, and in the perfect harmony that subsists among all ranks."*

Cook may have been right about submissive compliance, but "perfect harmony"? Well, he should have looked again, because the place was ravaged by rebellion and regicide (the murder of kings). In fact, they had to settle things by coming up with two coexisting leaders: a *Tu'i Tonga* to handle ceremonial duties, and a *Tu'i Ha'atakalau'a* to be the active ruler. (Sound familiar?) And they kept peace—some of the time!—by arranging marriages between the two ruling families. (Where have I heard that one before?)

The Tui Tonga...was a supreme and sacred ruler.... Sound like the divine right of kings?

Tonga has come a long way, much of the switch from ceremonial *garble* to *garb* thanks to the active leadership of the remarkable Tongan woman they called Queen Salote. When Salote died, the people of Tonga truly mourned her. She had "ruled" for forty-seven years and the changes that took place during her era were felt deeply and widely. The Old Treaty with Britain was replaced with a new one which no longer required that Tongans get advice from the British Consul on financial matters. A wider range of civil and criminal offences by foreigners could now be dealt with in Tongan courts. In contrast to the many annexations by European colonial powers in the South Pacific, Tonga remained an independent nation, and the government was almost entirely staffed by Tongan nationals.

"None of the most civilized nations have ever exceeded these islanders...in ready and submissive compliance with the commands of their chiefs."

Salote's achievements reflect not monarchy but citizenship. She cared about the people in her midst and committed herself to helping them. And given the tropical downpours in Tonga, I'm sure she got herself wet plenty of times in the process. By contrast, so voracious is the British appetite for the taste of royal blood that they take great pains to keep it from getting diluted with water. They display their kings and queens, princes and princesses, dukes and duchesses on covered balconies and sheltered reviewing stands, and relegate them to the insidious task of "being seen".

Garb to *garble*.... They just arrive, and claim they are the royalty from there!

"Some of the heathen Chiefs hate cannibalism, and I know several who could not be induced to taste human flesh. These, however, are rare exceptions to the rule. No one who is thoroughly acquainted with the Fijians, can say that this vitiated taste is not widely spread, or that there is not a large number who esteem such food a delicacy, giving it a decided preference above all other."

— Rev. Thomas Williams

Recipe # 9
THE DEEPEST CUT OF ALL

From SUBJECT
(the doer of an action)

To SUBJECTION
(submission to the
power and authority
of another)

It's springtime in Vancouver, 1993. A summit meeting is about to take place between two world leaders: Bill Clinton of the United States and Boris Yeltsin of Russia. The city is full of police and secret service agents—RCMP, CIA and KGB. There are between two and three thousand journalists from around the world here to cover the event. The punchline for hard news hounds is that the United States will hand over a $1.6 billion assistance package to bolster the free market system in Russia. It is dicey for the new American president because people back home are not too keen on giving money to the Russians. It is more dicey still for the new Russian president: he is facing an upcoming referendum on his leadership and people back home are not too keen on accepting charity from the Americans. Nevertheless, they are pushed into action, these two ordinary men from humble beginnings, because they are very clear about how they want to have their world.

But they'll have to push against the flow: not the flow of American sentiment about the Russians, nor the flow of hardline opposition to Yeltsin's brand of economic reform. No, they'll have to push against the flow of being two ordinary men from humble beginnings—for the world will not let them be ordinary.

The clues are in the news coverage. Reporters tell us when the two leaders will arrive and when they will depart, what motorcade routes they will likely take through the city, where they will dine and what will be on the menu (there's an interview with the chef), the rooms where they will meet and what will be in the rooms (there's an interview with the decorator), where they will take their walk, their jog, their boat ride: everywhere, in short, where we might catch a glimpse of two ordinary men from humble beginnings.

They'll have to push against the flow of being two ordinary men from humble beginnings.

People line the motorcade routes even though, for security reasons, the routes are only tentative. Some stay long hours in spite of pouring rain. One couple spends the entire day on the sidewalk so they can catch the entourage coming *and* going. A young school girl gets to shake hands with one of them. Displaying her palm to the camera, she declares, "I'll never wash it!"

There is *some* coverage about the substance of the summit, which consists mostly of journalists interviewing journalists. And there is a press conference at the end of it all: "What about the aid package?" they ask.

"It's a partnership, not a Christmas present."

"Is it big enough?"

"It's not too little, not too much."

They still haven't reported on Yeltsin's brand of economic reform—and that, it seems to me, is the critical issue. Is there anything there that will address rather than exacerbate the problems already inherent in both the Russian and American systems: unconstrained (state or private) capitalism, unlimited growth, economic disparity, concentration of wealth, environmental degradation, polluted lakes and rivers, clearcut forests, high unemployment, inner city decay, rampant crime, crisis in health care, drugs, alcohol, heart disease, cancer, headaches, sleeping disorders...?

They do report that Clinton goes jogging on the seawall at Stanley Park wearing a UBC sweatshirt and that he later spends $200 on souvenirs. He buys mugs and T-shirts. He puts it on his American Express card (they take a close-up shot of the American Express bill). The clerk gives him a form so he can claim his rebate on the goods and services tax—available to foreign visitors. They interview the clerk; she doesn't know whether or not he will fill in the form....

Two ordinary men, pressed into the service of being...what? Of being...archetypes—from *arche* (the ultimate of a kind) and *type* (an example or model): "an original model after which other similar things are patterned". Now if you want to achieve something in life, one of the best ways to advance toward your goal is to find someone who is the ultimate of that kind, and use this person as a role model. You swing into action, patterning yourself on the qualities and attributes that produce the desired results.

What do we do instead? Rather than being the doers of action, the subjects of our own lives, we *subject* ourselves to those who possess the very qualities and attributes we could otherwise develop in ourselves. It is interesting that Bill Clinton modelled himself on John Kennedy while others stood on the sidelines watching the presidential motorcade whiz by. Camelot! (I know it sounds a bit bizarre....)

Carl Jung says there are four levels of archetypes, each with a male and female component. Level 1 is the wholly physical man (like Tarzan) and the primitive woman (like in a Gauguin painting). It represents purely instinctual biological attraction. Level 2 is the romantic man (like the poet Shelley) and the aesthetic woman (Elizabeth Taylor). It represents a sexual, emotional level of development. Level 3 is the bearer of the word (Churchill) and spiritual devotion (Joan of Arc). It moves into the arena of moral and sacred conviction. Level 4 is the wise spiritual guide (Gandhi) and transcendent wisdom (Mother Teresa), who represent spiritual truth and insight, the final stage of development.

When we find someone in our midst who qualifies as an archetype at one of these levels, there is a strong tendency for psychological subjection, as in our response to Clinton and Yeltsin, bearers of the word, who represent a level 3 moral conviction. If a person qualifies at more than one level, the stage is set for a widescale psychological sellout, such as the (level 2) aesthetic Jacqueline Kennedy and Diana Spencer who acquire additional archetypal value with the (level 3) roles of "First Lady" and "Princess of Wales".

When we find someone in our midst who qualifies as an archetype...there is a strong tendency for psychological subjection.

Our willingness to subject ourselves to the authority of archetypal personalities is really an excuse for not taking action in our own right. Indeed, we gravitate to such people with the expectation, albeit unconscious, that we can realize our fantasies through them. So commonplace is this addiction to vicarious experience that we continually search out possible new candidates and press them into archetypal service.

This tendency is evident at the summit. Even the hype of two world leaders in the same place at the same time cannot satisfy the voracious psychological appetite. It all spills out innocently enough when a Canadian journalist interviews "the voice of America", ABC's Peter Jennings (who just happens to be Canadian) about the big event. "This is not the most exciting summit we have ever been to," confesses the famous news anchor. "For one thing, it is no longer a summit in the era of confrontation. So on a scale of one to ten, it's a summit down around three or four. There's a great deal of interest in the United States at the moment in Kim Campbell," he continues. "I noticed her picture in *Time* magazine. We've already assigned a reporter to try and do a piece on her."

Who's Kim Campbell?

Canada's Minister of Defence.

What's so interesting about that?

Well, she's running for the leadership of the Progressive Conservative party and if she wins, she'll be the next Prime Minister.

Aren't there a number of candidates running?

Well, yeah.

So?

She's a woman.

Oh.

And she has blonde hair.

Aha.

And when she was Minister of Justice, she posed for a photograph holding her legal gown in front of what appeared to be her naked body.

Whoa....

You could see her bare shoulders. No bra straps or nothin'.

More. More. We want more....

If we can plop a bare-shouldered blonde in the role of prime minister, we can settle back and enjoy the show without ever having to decide how to have a world.

She runs down a corridor in Ottawa; the press is there. She arrives at the airport in Vancouver; the press is there. She lays a wreath at a cenotaph in England; the press is there. Anywhere, in short, where we might catch a glimpse of..."the Madonna of Canadian politics". In other words, a double archetype. If we can plop a bare-shouldered blonde in the role of prime minister, we can settle back and enjoy the show without ever having to decide how to have a world.

Subject to *subjection:* the ultimate self-sabotage, the deepest cut of all.... Such is the power of archetypes. And so reluctant are we to relinquish them that we cannot let go even when they die. Elvis lives. So does John Kennedy, and Princess Grace, and Marilyn Monroe....

"When the slain are few, and fall into the hands of the victors, it is the rule to eat them.... But when a large party can get but one or two bodies, every part is consumed."

— Rev. Thomas Williams

Recipe # 10
SEVERING THE LIMBS

From ARMS
(the upper limbs of the human body)

To ARMAMENTS
(equipment of war)

I am in Australia as a consultant for the United Nations Pavilion at World Expo 88. The locals are curious about the upcoming fair and want to find out about it. On this occasion I have been invited to a city college to speak at their graduation ceremony. It happens to be the day before Good Friday. The students and faculty are sitting here, waiting for the ceremony to end so they can break for the holiday. It is pouring rain and I am talking to them about death and destruction.

"Not a very fitting way to start an Easter break!" I chide. "Or is it? In fact, maybe it's very fitting because if you think about it, the purpose of Good Friday is to remember a guy who got himself killed for calling God a four-letter word."

There is no reaction.

"What was the word?"

Silence.

"Does anybody know what the word is?"

Still no response. A nervous cough.

"What is the four-letter word that he said God is? God is...what?"

A faculty member whispers, "Love."

"...the purpose of Good Friday is to remember a guy who got himself killed for calling God a four-letter word."

"Yes," I say. "He said, 'God is love,' and I'm not surprised it didn't jump from your lips because the word is taboo. Have you noticed that people rarely talk about love? They talk about war and hate and violence but they hardly ever talk about love—and if you go around talking about love, people will start getting suspicious of you."

They're giggling now.

"I spent twelve years schooling and in all those years I never heard the word 'love' mentioned even once. It seems a rather important thing not to have learned anything about so I thought I would try again and I did twelve years of university. I studied the disciplines that should know something about it: Psychology, Philosophy, Anthropology— and I learned a little bit about love from each of them.

"I spent twelve years schooling and in all those years I never heard the word 'love' mentioned even once."

"In Psychology, I found that babies in an orphanage, when given proper physical care but no love, would mysteriously die. Four years of Psychology and that's what they told me about love. In Philosophy I found out the Greeks have a lot of words for it while we have only one. There's *agape,* godly love; *philios,* brotherly love; *eros,* sexual love.... That's what I got from Philosophy. Then in Anthropology I learned that when you introduce money into a traditional society, it makes possible love as a value in itself. Up to that point it doesn't come up—and doesn't need to—because people are tied to each other through a network of kinship obligations.

"So, as you can see, there hasn't been a lot of research

done about love—and yet it would seem to be a rather critical thing because if you don't get any of it, you can die (Psychology), and there are all kinds of it (Philosophy), and where there's love, there's money (Anthropology)."

They're laughing now.

"Well, the United Nations Pavilion is all about love but, of course, we never use the word because, remember, it's taboo...."

World Expo '88 opens and the months go by. In August, we have International Children's Week at the fair so we decide to feature children in the UN Pavilion. We dress them up in our hosting uniforms and have them greet the guests in the theatres, introduce the presentations and press the buttons to start the computers. Who says kids can't run the show! Mind you, they are only 12 years old, and when they stretch out their arms to point to the exits, the sleeves on their Ken Done sweatshirts almost cover their fingertips. The audience laughs—but they get the message.

Well, the other thing we have these "Youth Ambassadors" do is conduct a survey on the Expo site to find out what kids their age think about the world and about their own future. Interestingly, the boys interview boys and the girls interview girls. If they had been a couple of years older, it would probably have been the other way around! Anyway, what they find out is that the big thing on kids' minds is war, especially nuclear war. In other words, their big concern about the future is that there isn't going to be one! That's not a lot of incentive for busting your brains in school!

This planet is our house, and by conservative estimate we still have at least 30,000 nuclear weapons in it. Children do not deserve to grow up in a home like that. We are unfit parents.

They have other concerns as well. Some kids are worried there won't be a job for them when they grow up. Imagine! In an abundant land like Australia, to be afraid you will grow up and live in poverty! There are a few whose big concern is loneliness. They are afraid they will grow up to be lonely. Imagine, being lonely on a planet with five billion unique and mostly interesting people. ("And even the dull have their story.")

Then there are a few wild cards, like the ten-year-old whose biggest concern about the future is that she won't get into law school. At ten years of age, she's worried about getting into law school! There is a twelve-year-old boy whose biggest concern about the future is—get this!—marriage—afraid that he will, not that he won't. Actually, he is not an Aussie kid; he's from New York, and his fear is probably well placed given the price of divorce lawyers in that town.

Well, those are the unusual ones, but the majority of kids—and they interviewed more than 600 of them—are concerned about nuclear war. These results are consistent with studies conducted in other parts of the world. Children in Australia, like children in Canada, in the United States of America, or in the (former) Soviet Union, are afraid we are going to drop the big one.

In one survey, a young American boy is asked what he thinks about nuclear bombs. He says, "They're bad. They're really bad. In fact, they're so bad that you wouldn't even want to have one in your house." Well, this planet is our house, and by conservative estimate we still have at least 30,000 nuclear weapons in it. Children do not deserve to grow up in a home like that. We are unfit parents.

Let's just look at how we've put our house in order. In 1986, which was, ironically, the International Year of Peace, global military expenditures reached $900 billion per year. It's now over a trillion. That's a million million dollars every year on the preparation for and execution of war—more than $2 million every minute! All this while one adult in 3 cannot read or write and one billion people live in inadequate housing. That's not even the worst of it. While there are enough grains in stock on the planet to feed the world's hungry, the total number of hungry people is still rising. Almost one-fifth of the world's population do not eat sufficient calories for an active working day.

What a fascinating paradox! A species hell-bent on destroying itself when survival is the name of the game. It's not as if we don't have the brains to figure it out. In fact, we've got three of them, all designed to maximize our chances of survival and minimize our chances of extinction. There's the reptilian stem (limbic node) which is over 500 million years old. It's concerned with basic biological stability, like breathing. It's also concerned with "fight or flight" survival reactions. Then there's the mammalian brain, dating from 300-200 million years ago, that sits on top of the limbic node. It looks after things like metabolism and hormones. It's also busy with another basic survival function—territoriality. Finally there's the cerebral cortex, a more recent system, showing up around 50 million years ago. It's about the size of a crumpled up double sheet of newsprint, precariously layered over the other two brains. Incidentally, if you were to spread out that newsprint, only one column would be dedicated to rational thought—which covers almost everything we think we know. We've only just begun to tap into the potential of the cerebral cortex. Maybe there's a *love* column in there....

In...the International Year of Peace, global military expenditures reached $900 billion per year...more than $2 million every minute!

The bottom line is that the "brain" is not designed primarily for thinking—and thinking is not its chief interest in any case. It is playing the survival game, and it will "survive" (i.e. protect or defend) whatever it thinks that it is (i.e. how it identifies itself): as an individual, a family, a clan, a tribe, a ·religious sect, a nation.... That's why we can get people to build bombs, withhold food, go to war.... They are "surviving" whatever they think they are: Christian, Muslim, Catholic, Protestant, Russian, American, Canadian, Quebecois.... It's not about thinking or intelligence or rationality. It's not even about good or bad, right or wrong. It's about looking out for whatever we think we are.

It seems to me that if we want to have life for ourselves and for our children, we had better get it into our heads that *what we are is one human family,* and we had better be clear that *our home is the whole planet,* because whatever we think we are, that is what we will protect and defend—and we will destroy anything that even appears to get in the way.

What a fascinating paradox! A species hell-bent on destroying itself when survival is the name of the game.

The old American cartoon character Pogo put it this way: "We have seen the enemy—and he is us."

Maybe it's high time we started using that four-letter word!

 *"Would that this horrible record could be finished here! but the vakatotoga, the torture, must be noticed. Nothing short of the most fiendish cruelty could dictate some of these forms of torment, the worst of which consists in cutting off parts and even limbs of the victim while still living, and cooking them and eating them before his eyes, sometimes finishing the brutality by offering him his own cooked flesh to eat."*

—Rev. Thomas Williams

Recipe #11
TRIMMING THE FAT

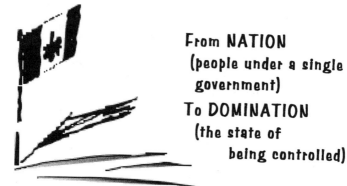

From **NATION**
(people under a single government)

To **DOMINATION**
(the state of being controlled)

It is Saturday, October 24, 1992—game six of the World Series. A Canadian team is in the play-offs for the first time in baseball history. Never mind that none of the players is actually Canadian; they're almost all Americans but they're playing for the Toronto Blue Jays and that makes them "our" team. They're leading the series three games to two and if they can clinch tonight's win against the Atlanta Braves they will emerge "world" champions!

They played our national anthem in Atlanta the other day with the Canadian flag hanging upside down.

Canadian prestige is at stake, and Canadian power, and Canadian pride. Our national identity is also on the line: it's our chance to rank number one, in spite of our Prime Minister's recent public statement that the United States is the most important country in the world. His comment is not the only blow to the Canadian psyche of late. The whole country is reeling from economic setbacks, job losses and social upheaval on a scale not seen since the dirty thirties, as it tries to adjust to a new Free Trade Agreement with the United States, introduced by a government with the support of only a minority of voters. So much national self-determination was traded away in this agreement that it prompted one former trade negotiator to comment that if it had come about as a result of war, it would have been the greatest defeat Canada had ever suffered.

To add to this affront to democracy, the same ruling party is now pushing ahead with a North American Free Trade Agreement in the midst of strong public opposition, with limited parliamentary debate and no referendum. Canadians are watching their country go down the tube....

Now, maybe the Blue Jays can assuage our psyche and restore us to greatness and national purpose. Then our politicians will listen to us, eh! Maybe the Americans will learn something about us too: they played our national anthem in Atlanta the other day with the Canadian flag hanging upside down!

Yup, this ball game is comin' just in time because it's on the heels of a very long drawn-out campaign to amend the country's constitution. The government of the day is making a really big deal about it—and because we are a democracy, they're going to put it to a national referendum. Never mind that they've spent $7.2 million on the campaign telling us to vote "yes"—and never mind that we will eventually find out $7.1 million of that money came from giant, largely American-owned, corporations. Some kind of democracy!

"So much national self-determination was traded away...that if it had come about as a result of war, it would have been the greatest defeat Canada had ever suffered."

But that's not until Monday. Tonight—Saturday—the eyes of Canada are glued to television sets from St. John's to Victoria as the Blue Jays battle for the trophy.

Me? I'm at the opera. Verdi's *Rigoletto*, adapted from Victor Hugo's *"Le Roi s'amuse"*. It's about a Duke who misuses his power. Actually, it's about a society that grants power to a Duke and then allows him to abuse it. It is also about a court jester who tries to rid the world of the Duke.

The opening scene sets the stage: a palace ball where the flirtatious Duke rejoices in libertine hedonism. He is "what the music says he is: aristocratic, charming, elegant—and exceedingly unprincipled". By the end of Act I, he has professed his love to Rigoletto's beautiful daughter, Gilda.

Intermission: patrons wander from the theatre and mingle in the foyer; I step outside for a breath of cool autumn air. When we take our seats again, there is a message on the super-title screen above the stage: "The game is tied at two in the bottom of the tenth." The audience takes a collective breath.

Act II: the conflict unfolds. The Duke makes advances to Gilda, and Rigoletto conspires to get rid of the Duke. The second act ends, the curtain closes, the audience claps appreciably.... Suddenly a new message appears on the super-title screen: "Toronto Blue Jays: 1992 World Series Champs!"

Well, this sophisticated audience of socially-correct opera buffs goes wild with shouts and vigorous hand clapping. A lady sitting behind me utters, "We've waited a long time for this."

We have?

I wonder what she means by "this"?

I wonder what she means by "we"?

In the final act Rigoletto hires an assassin to do away with the Duke—but circumstances alter events and the assassin, exercising his own capacity for chicanery, chooses a substitute victim. When Rigoletto returns at midnight to dump what he thinks is the Duke's body into the river, he hears—off in the distance—the Duke's voice! Astonished, he opens the sack and finds...the body of his own daughter!

Verdi was a master of social analysis and human expression. He often used his music to express his sentiments against tyranny and to advocate liberty. Thanks to his own humble beginnings in a small Italian village, he understood the concerns of the common man. He was also conscious of his competence as a composer and disliked with passion deferring to people with superior political or social rank—especially when he knew their talents to be inferior to his own.

Verdi's social philosophy is not lost on this production of

the opera. In the *Director's Notes*, I read, "What we are presented with is a society which has gone wrong, which presents its members little choice but to act in predetermined ways. I get the sense that if we were to rid Rigoletto's world of this Duke, another just as amoral would take his place.... Working on this production has made me think again that perhaps we err in expending our rage on the Dukes of the world when our anger should be focussed on the society that creates them...."

Next day, the Toronto Blue Jays return to a hero's welcome. Canadians bask in glory and national pride. The day after that, the nation takes part in the other diversion—voting in a referendum that has little to do with their economic setbacks, job losses and social upheaval. Meanwhile, the real forces that are trimming the fat of Canadians continue unnoticed and unchecked.

A letter to the editor in the next *Maclean's*, a national news magazine, demonstrates just how easily people can be taken in. "In the course of one week," suggests the writer, "a baseball team was able to do what countless politicians have not been capable of since Canada was conceived—unite Canadians." As though this were what nationhood is about!

How willingly we grant power to a Duke and allow him to abuse it! How willingly we occupy ourselves with diversions! How willingly we slip from *nation* to *domination!* "Perhaps we err in expending our rage on the Dukes of the world when our anger should be focussed on the society that creates them."

"Last Monday afternoon...a report came that some dead men were being brought here.... Almost before we had time to think, the men were laid on the ground before our house, and Chiefs and priests and people met to divide them to be eaten."

—Rev. Thomas Williams

Recipe # 12

TAKING A SLICE OUT OF THEM

From PERSON
(an individual)

To PERSONA
(what an individual
appears to be)

I'm beginning an anthropological field study in a small village on a remote island in Fiji. It's Sunday and my young research assistant, Tau—who is also a lay preacher—is to give a sermon this afternoon in a neighbouring village. I want very much to document his presentation so I ask if I might accompany him. He hesitates but finally agrees to take me.

En route he says not a word to me: he just stares straight ahead, walking at a vigorous pace. I would conclude he doesn't like me except for the fact he appears to be deep in thought. I surmise he is mentally delivering his sermon so I make a point of not disturbing him.

After a considerable length of time, he breaks the silence: "The reason I acted like I didn't want to bring you is not because I didn't want you to come. It's because this is when I practise my sermons out loud and I can't do it in front of anyone."

"Yes, you can. Go ahead; I won't pay any attention."

He reflects for a moment, then he breaks into his monologue with all the courage and conviction of a Methodist missionary. There we are, the two of us, walking along the road, he now bellowing his message and swinging his arms in the air, I now carrying his Bible in silence.

A while later we spot a solitary figure approaching in the distance. The sermon stops abruptly and Tau is silent once again. When the man gets within speaking distance, the two of them exchange customary Fijian greetings. *"Bula. Lesu mai vei? "* ("Hello. Where do you come from?")

Then the most curious thing happens: they start to laugh—and they laugh and laugh. They slap each other on the back—and they laugh some more and slap some more. This goes on for some time; I just can't figure out what is so funny.

They say good-bye and go their separate ways. Tau resumes his serious mood instantly. Curiosity gets the better of me. "You must really like that guy a lot," I say to him. "The two of you have such a great time together."

"Never saw him before in my life," comes the reply. "He's from Navosa-Nadroga and I'm from Lomaiviti, and we have a joking relationship." He continues with his sermon.

How strange...how imprisoning, to have your relationships so prescribed that you cannot act naturally.

I recall being with Tau on another occasion. We were returning to the village from the yam gardens along a trail cut through the jungle when another man approached; this time it was his older brother. As soon as they spotted each other, they dropped their eyes and continued walking as though the other were not present. On that narrow jungle path, they managed to maneuver so as not even to brush against each other. Once the older brother was a short distance away, Tau said to me, "Please run back and tell him he can take some yams from my garden."

Now, Tau is 27 years old and his older brother is 33. In all those years they have never spoken to each other. In the language of Anthropology, they observe a strict avoidance relationship. How strange, I think, how imprisoning, to have your relationships so prescribed that you cannot act naturally. Culture—dictating when you must speak and when you must not speak, when you must joke and when you must not joke, when you must defer and when you must not defer.... It all turns on who you are and where you fit into the social hierarchy. Their culture is slicing them into fragmented human beings, like actors wearing masks to indicate the roles they are playing. Why don't they just quit acting and get real?

The answer, of course, is that to them, it *is* real. They don't know it's just a social construction of reality and that they are *persons* turned into *personas*. They haven't read Carl Jung; they don't know that a persona is nothing real, that it's "just a compromise formation between an individual and society as to what a man should appear to be". They get a name, earn a title, perform a function: that's what they think is real—but in relation to their essential individuality, their *person*, it's only a *secondary* reality, created more by others than by themselves.*

It all turns on who you are and where you fit into the social hierarchy.

I can see the thatch huts of the neighbouring village through the palm trees now. Tau finishes his rehearsal and takes back his Bible. I'm still deep in thought. Amazing the way these people let somebody else tell them how they must or must not relate to another human being....

Then it strikes me: we do the same thing! The queen shakes our hand; we do not shake hers. She speaks to us and only then may we reply. If, per chance, we get an interview, we initially address her as "Your Majesty", and after that, we call her "Ma'am". We address others as "Your Worship", "Your Holiness", "Reverend", "Doctor", "Professor", but not "Farmer", "Plumber", or "Carpenter". We call our teachers by their surnames, but they need not do the same for us. It all turns on who we are and where we fit into the social hierarchy. We let our culture take a slice out of us and then wonder why we feel like fragmented human beings.

Hmmm...

We are about to enter the village. Tau now informs me I will give a sermon as well! It is something expected of visitors, he says, and it would be considered unfriendly of me not to do it. It doesn't need to be long, he adds, and I can deliver it in English; he will translate.

What a great time to tell me—after he has had a nice long practice period, with me carrying his Bible! But, culturally speaking, I know I've got to do it—and I had better think up something really fast. It will need to be prepackaged, sort of like the sermon equivalent of a TV dinner.

I'm called to the pulpit. I look down on a sea of flashing white teeth, dark eyes and masses of thick black curly hair. They are a handsome people. I launch into my little sermon.

"Let me be an instrument of peace."

Tau repeats the words in Fijian.

"Where there is hatred, let me sow love...

I proceed a line at a time, pausing for the translation.

"Where there is injury, pardon...

The congregation nods with approval and appreciation.

"Where there is doubt, faith...

"Where there is despair, hope...

"Where there is darkness, light...

"And where there is sadness, joy...."

Yup. The Peace Prayer of St. Francis. I don't exactly tell them that's what it is. They are very Protestant and this could be construed as being very Catholic.

"...May I not so much seek to be consoled as to console....

"To be understood as to understand...

"To be loved as to love...."

They like it.

"For it is in giving that we receive....

"It is in pardoning that we are pardoned....

"And it is in dying that we are born to eternal life...."

But do they get it?

Get real!

 "So far as I can learn, this abominable food is never eaten raw, although the victim is often presented in full life and vigour. "

—Rev. Thomas Williams

Recipe # 13
EAT YOUR HEART OUT

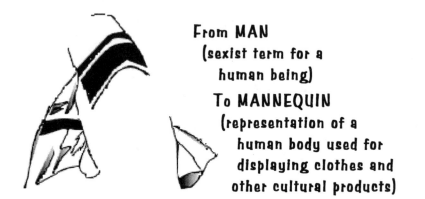

From **MAN**
(sexist term for a
human being)

To **MANNEQUIN**
(representation of a
human body used for
displaying clothes and
other cultural products)

It is 1975. I am living in Calcutta, studying at the Ramakrishna Mission Institute of Culture. Just a short distance away is the convent where Mother Teresa lives with her Sisters of Charity. A group of children in Canada has raised some money for Mother Teresa's home for abandoned children and I go to deliver it to her on their behalf.

I present myself at the convent on Lower Circular Road at six o'clock in the morning as prearranged. The outside of the building is unimpressive and gives no hint as to the hum of activity taking place inside. Young women move about, dressed in the now familiar habit: white cotton with a blue band. There are about fifty of them, one of whom ushers me into a clean and sparsely-furnished room. While I wait for Mother Teresa, I watch a number of these graceful figures washing laundry in the courtyard below. They are singing, the bending of their bodies keeping pace with the rhythm of the music: a song to God for the heart and soul of humanity. Off to one side in a chapel I hear the sound of morning prayers.

Mother Teresa enters, small, aged, even frail—yet she moves and speaks with undeniable strength and tenacity. In her, one meets the whole person: physical, mental, emotional and spiritual qualities that add up to...beauty. Timeless beauty, a beauty that permeates. It radiates from the form of this small, aged woman to the outer walls of the convent, from the convent into the streets of Calcutta, from Calcutta across the plains of India, from India to every continent of the world.... Never did the words of the poet ring more true to me: "A thing of beauty is a joy forever...".

In her, one meets the whole person: physical, mental, emotional and spiritual qualities that add up to...beauty.

Years later, I am home in Vancouver watching one of those annual beauty contests on television. Not a pageant, they caution at the outset, because a pageant is a parade. This is more than a pageant; it's a competition. Fifty-some "beautiful, intelligent and definitely women of the nineties" *(sic)* bidding for the title of "Miss World America". A brand new title because "to be physically beautiful is just not enough anymore". This time the judges will be looking for that combination of physical, mental, emotional and spiritual qualities that would make a fine "Miss World". "Total personality" and "beauty with a purpose"—brought to you by a breakfast cereal and a toilet bowl cleaner.

The contest begins. The setting is impressive: a big stage and a live television audience. The contestants are introduced. They're dressed in "the red, white and blue", divided into four categories: "cowgirls" from the southwest (no skirts); "Southern belles" from the southeast (their skirts fall off when they stand up); "Indians" from the northwest (big, tall feathers); and "Yankee Doodle dandies" from the northeast (big tall hats and not much more). They are singing, the bending of their bodies keeping pace with the rhythm of the music: a song to the star-spangled banner for the heart and soul of America. Off to one side, the host announces there's a cash prize of $100,000 for the winner.

A commercial break: there's a secret formula for cutting grease, something for getting rid of pet odours in your carpet, a potion to help you digest dairy products, a frosted breakfast cereal and a toothpaste.

Ten semifinalists are chosen. Then a new kind of swimsuit competition: no heels—they're in their bare feet. We see the body and we hear the mind. "Giving: that's how you learn and that's how you grow," echoes one of the hopefuls.

More commercials: a feminine hygiene product, for *real* protection; a packaged breakfast cereal, sugar-frosted; a deodorant, for those stressful moments; a vacuum cleaner, all parts attached. A fast food outlet, selling time; a soft drink, selling taste; and a drug store, selling everything.... Nothing of use to Mother Teresa here.

Now come the interviews—with serious questions this time, they promise. What about women's rights? Social programs? Okay, gun control? Next, we get a prepackaged insert about how the contestants spent their week: fun events intermingled with serious sessions on modelling, makeup and hair styling. And they attended lectures: the topics were women's rights, social programs and gun control!

"And a word from our sponsors." A salad dressing, an eye cleanser, a laundry detergent—and, this time, a *portable* vacuum cleaner.

A fast food outlet, selling time; a soft drink, selling taste; and a drug store, selling everything.

The evening gown competition is next. Nothing in white cotton with a blue band here.

A bathroom cleaner, something for yeast infection and vaginal itch, a breakfast bar, potpourri for pet odours—and a douche. Gee, I wonder who their audience is?

We meet the five finalists.

A home perm, a hot oil treatment, another deodorant, another cereal, another product for yeast infection.

The booty includes: "a crown jewel collection created for her royal patronage"; a year's supply of groceries (shopping carts plumb full of soft drinks, quick oats, pickles, more soft drinks, corn pops, processed cereal, chocolate sauce, canned beans and corn); a winter ski vacation in Colorado; a full-length black mink coat, a lamb coat with fox collar and a mink section jacket; swim wear and a year's supply of tanning products; contemporary fashions including everything from a military jacket to cowboy boots; lingerie; a year's supply of hair care products; a year of "study" in fashion design and retail marketing; a mohair wardrobe; a year's supply of home perm; sophisticated fashions and a diamond-studded crown ring—"These gifts and more just for being named 1992 Miss World America."

A nutri-grain bar, a pregnancy test, something for athlete's foot, bath soap. Another product for yeast infection? Oh, a different brand which is "more than just a cure". (Really?)

Miss Florida wins. She's mannequin of the year.

To the other fifty hopefuls who strutted their all, who taped their tits for better cleavage, who sprayed stikum on their bums to keep their swimsuits in place, who greased their teeth to get maximum mileage from that constant smile...well, eat your hearts out!

And to all those women in the television audience who yearn to be "mannequins in their own image", who rush out and buy the products to enhance what nature did—or who have cosmetic surgery to correct what nature did not—well, eat *your* hearts out too!

Mother Teresa, where are you when we need you?

"I never saw a body baked whole, but have most satisfactory testimony that, on the island of Ngau, and one or two others, this is really done. The body is first placed in a sitting position, and, when taken from the oven, is covered with black powder, surmounted with a wig, and paraded about as if possessed with life."

—Rev. Thomas Williams

Recipe # 14

BITE YOUR TONGUE

From LANGUE
(language)

To LANGUISH
(to lose strength)

I am sitting in the restaurant of a five-star hotel in Port Vila, the capital of Vanuatu, which used to be known as the New Hebrides. Or should I say Les Nouveaux Hebrides, for the country was a colonial condominium sporting two foreign governments and, like back home in Canada, two codes of law, and two official languages: English and French. Some people speak one and some the other, and then there are a few who speak both, so you never quite know in which language someone is going to address you.

On this occasion, the hostess comes over to my table and says, *"Yu alrite?"* I'm puzzled by the question at first. Then I realize she's speaking not English—or French—but the current official language of Vanuatu known as Bislama or Pidgin, and she's asking simply and politely, "How are you?"

Cute, eh! Like the little sign on the carefully tended lawn around the hotel compound: *"No woka abaot long gras."*

It takes a while for Pidgin to "take"—and that includes "taking it seriously". That's because sometimes it sounds rather funny. The Pidgin rendering of the "Prince of Wales" is *nambawan pikinini blong Kwin* (number one pickaninny belong Queen). A piano is described as a *bigfala bokis blong waetman, tut blong em sam i blak, sam i waet; taem yu kilim emi singaot* (big European box, with some white and some black teeth; when you strike it, it sings out). A violin is *smol sista blong bigfala bokis sipos yu skrasem bel blong em i krae* (little sister to the piano; if you scratch its belly, it cries).

It takes a while for Pidgin to "take"—and that includes "taking it seriously".

There are lots of little signs here and there that sound rather amusing too, like this one at a book exchange: *Sipos yu takem wan buk yu putum wan buk bakagen*. That's clear enough. This warning about shoplifting posted in a duty free store on the main street in Port Vila is a bit tougher:

> *LUKAOT*
>
> *Stil long stoa hemi wan trabol.*
> *Bae mifala i singaot i Polis sapos*
> *yu stil, no mata hamas yia yu kat.*

Here's another one—from the airline, Vanair, warning that it is an offence to write graffiti on company property, and that offenders will be prosecuted by the police:

> *PABLIK NOTIS*
>
> *Yu no mas raet long eni samting long*
> *plen frum em properti blong Vanair.*
> *Sapos yu no respectim law ia, bae*
> *mifala i putum long hand blong ol polis.*

It gets easy, almost infectious, after awhile. There's *plis* (please) and *tangkyu tumas* (thank-you very much), *lukim yu* (see you later) and *hareap plis* (please hurry). It's everywhere: in the newspapers, on the radio, in Parliament, and in the streets. Here's what is written on my airline boarding pass: *Plis givim kad ia befo yu go insaed long plen*. There are subtle distinctions, like the difference between *kilim* (to hit, to strike), and *kilim i ded* (to kill). Fun, eh! And there are funnier ones still, like the rendering of the word "bra" as *basket blong titi*.

Fun and funny, that is, until you find out a bit more about why the *Ni Vanuatu,* as the people here choose to be called, speak to each other in this English-based *lingua franca.*

It all started in the early nineteenth century when Melanesians worked aboard European whaling ships and needed a way to communicate with their bosses. The same thing later applied with the traders of sandalwood and *beche de mer.* By the middle of the century, all those industries were winding down and new ones were taking their place, the most critical of which was the sugar cane industry. Cheap labour was needed for the plantations in Queensland, Australia, and Melanesia was the nearest available source. Between 1863 and 1911 more than 50,000 *Ni Vanuatu* were recruited to work the cane fields; "blackbirding", they called it.

Pidgin is anything but amusing to them.

Once in Australia, recruits from the same island and language group were separated so they could not communicate with each other and "cause trouble". As a result, these indentured workers were forced to speak to each other in the jargon of Pidgin English which was reinforced by the spoken English of their bosses and plantation owners. When they returned home years later, the Melanesians passed on the jargon English to their relatives and villages. And in a country like Vanuatu which has a distinct language for every 1200 people, a *lingua franca* that marries basic English word sounds with Melanesian grammar is no laughing matter.

Vanuatu received its independence from British and French colonial masters in 1980. Now, through Bislama—funny as it may sound to the European ear—distinct language and cultural groups communicate together. It's a remarkable achievement for a remote country in a corner of the South Pacific with 130,000 people on 80 islands speaking more than a hundred distinct languages. I'm sure Pidgin is anything but amusing to them.

Less amusing still is the fact that Canadians, with their similar English and French heritage—who have had independence for almost one and a half centuries—continue to wrangle about their two official (imported) languages as though there were no native groups in the territory! Canada's aboriginal peoples are scattered across the vast continent of North America, separated from each other by culture and geography, with no *lingua franca* to "cause trouble". And cause trouble they might, for most of them live in appalling poverty in this rich country. They have had their lands swindled from them, their means of livelihood dismantled, and their laws and codes of conduct undermined by colonial masters who stayed on.

In short, they are left to languish—that is, until someone of special importance visits the country, notably members of the British royal family. That's when the natives are paraded out to dance on *nambawan graon blong Kwin* (Crown land) and to *givim Kwin wan samting olgeta mekem* (something they made themselves)—another native artifact!

Canadians continue to wrangle about their two official (imported) languages as though there were no native groups in the territory!

Yumitufela (you-me-two fellow, i.e. "we") *ni Kanata* (of Canada)...*gat sam nogud kastom.*

"*The practice of kidnapping persons, on purpose to be eaten, proves that this flesh is in high repute. I have conversed with those who had escaped, severely wounded, from an attempt to steal them, as a supply for a forthcoming feast; and one of the last bodies which I saw offered to a Chief was thus obtained for the special entertainment of the distinguished Visitor.*"

—Rev. Thomas Williams

Recipe # 15
GETTING THEM INTO HOT WATER

From PATH
(a trodden way)

To PATHOGEN
(an agent that causes disease)

I am on a remote island in Fiji. It's very early on in my field-work for my anthropological studies. It's Sunday, *Siga Tabu* in Fijian which translates as "Taboo Day"—the day you're not allowed to do much of anything. It's a paradox, when you think about it, because it's the one day in seven set aside to *re-create* ourselves so that we may "have life and have it abundantly". Here, on this high volcanic island surrounded by a brilliant coral reef, it would be a wonderful time to swim in the fresh water stream that flows down into the ocean, or watch the brightly-coloured fish weave among the corals, or climb the stately palm trees to twist off some sweet-tasting coconuts....

But when in Fiji, do as the Fijians do—so I put away my fieldwork materials and "rest" inside my thatch hut.... Without any prompting, the children of the village soon fill my little hut to overflowing. They sit and chat; they lie down and nap; and they "read" my books and look at my magazines, oftentimes staring at the pictures upside down.

On one occasion, something tickles the funny-bones of these culturally-uninitiated kids and they start to laugh. It's wonderful to hear children laugh; they are so spontaneous. Very soon, however, a village elder pokes his head in the doorway, looks at the children, then at me and, with a grimace on his face, declares, "Pamela, the children are laughing!"

"Yes", I reply. "The children are laughing."

"It's Sunday," he continues.

"Yes, it's Sunday."

He stares at the children. Their laughter stops. Silence. Sunday! *Siga Tabu.* Now I get it: the children are not supposed to laugh on Sunday! How stupid of me! How culturally insensitive! Here I am getting these innocent little children into hot water!

Then I think, no! It's not I who's getting them into hot water. It's their culture. I mean, how could these people get so far away from the point of it all! Something as natural as laughter, and children are not even allowed to express it! Don't they realize what happens when you restrain someone from expressing an emotion! If you don't allow expression, you get suppression, or depression, or repression. It's the perfect recipe for making things go really haywire.

How did they end up with such a weird take on what this guy Jesus was trying to get into people's heads! Doesn't his message translate into this culture? Surely, his whole point was to express human nature—and these people are doing just the opposite.

Then I realize it's not that the message doesn't translate into *this* culture. It doesn't translate into *any* culture because the whole point of culture is to harness human energy and to put it to "productive" use. The Church is a willing participant in this conspiracy. Not only that, the professional Christians who are supposed to be offering us the definitive statement on our expressed humanity are often the ones with the most screwed-up take of all.

It's not that the message doesn't translate into this culture. It doesn't translate into any culture.

Take, for example, the position of the Catholic Church on celibacy. Its clergy is denied the natural expression of their human sexuality. Then, when they get themselves into hot water, which they do and they will, they are removed from their posts and thrust into jails. Think about it: a culture that first locks individuals into emotional prisons and then responds by locking them into physical ones! It's a classic case of being starved and then accused of being sick.

The whole point of abstaining from sexual activity in the spiritual sense is not to *deny* expression of sexual drive but to *sublimate* it into ever-higher states of consciousness. According to kundalini yoga, it's a process of moving energy up the spine, through "The Great Chain"—the seven major chakras (stages or levels), the locations of which are not only symbolic but actual. The first chakra (anal) represents *matter* (as in faecal matter); the second, *sex* (genitals); the third, *emotions* (gut reactions); the fourth, *love and belongingness* (heart); the fifth, *discursive intellect* (voice box); the sixth, *higher mental-psychic powers* (neocortex); the seventh, at and beyond the brain itself, *transcendence*.

There is nothing mysterious or occult about all this—but to do it, first you have to withdraw from the world and remove yourself from your network of social relationships. Otherwise, you're playing with fire.

Instead, what does the Catholic Church do to its clergy? It suppresses their natural sexual expression while, at the same time, throwing them into the social thick of things.

Like these innocent Fijian children, the poor priests haven't got a chance. When they screw up—literally—the very culture that got them into hot water turns cold on them.

"Lord, have mercy", 'cause they take your path and turn it into a pathogen. And even on weekdays, that's no laughing matter.

"*The manner in which the poor wretches were treated was most shamefully disgusting.... When they took them away to be cooked, they dragged them on the ground; one had a rope round his neck, and the others they took by the hands and feet....*"
—Rev. Thomas Williams

Recipe # 16
KEEPING THE LID ON

From CULT
(devotion to a person
or ideal)

To CULTURE
(socially transmitted
behavior)

His European name is Pierre and he speaks not a word of English. That is not to say he is deficient in languages, however, for he is fluent in three of them: first, that of his village at Sulphur Bay on the island of Tanna in the former "New Hebrides"; second, Bislama, the Pidgin English which is the official language of his country, now called Vanuatu; and finally, French, another legacy of the colonial condominium (or, as the locals call it, "pandemonium") government set up by France and England, which plagued his native land until as recently as 1980.

A small wooden model airplane marks the entrance to Pierre's village which is itself enclosed in a "stockade" of crude wooden posts.

I have come to Pierre's village to witness firsthand a Melanesian phenomenon commonly known as a "cargo cult". A cargo cult is a religious movement where participants engage in a number of strange and exotic rituals in order to gain possession of "European" goods. These goods, known as cargo, or "kago" in Pidgin, refer to imported items such as tinned food, rice, axes, firearms, knives, cloth, and the like.

Typically, a cargo cult is founded and led by a single prophet. He is usually a charismatic leader who takes what is valuable in his own culture and blends it with a vision of a hoped-for future. That future includes the superior standard of living he sees others enjoying—notably white Europeans parked on his soil—while his own people suffer economic and social powerlessness.

To achieve economic and social conditions that will "correct" the existing imbalance of power, the cultists start doing what they see the more successful Europeans doing. They march with "rifles", build "wharves" and "airstrips", listen to "radios", even talk on "telephones", believing that by so doing, the ships and airplanes will arrive, loaded with European goods. The problem is, of course, neither the prophet nor his followers are aware of how the world works outside their native Melanesia. Nor do they realize how powerful are the wealthy corporate elites at work inside their country. As a result, when the goods fail to arrive, the prophet—if not the whole cult—is found out, and one or the other is replaced by someone or something else. Once again, hopeful cult supporters will fall in line.

They march with "rifles", build "wharves" and "airstrips", listen to "radios", even talk on "telephones", believing that by so doing, the ships and airplanes will arrive, loaded with European goods.

Pierre's village, here at Sulphur Bay, is headquarters for one of the more enduring and notorious cults, the *John Frum* movement. No one is quite sure when this particular cult got started, but it was probably in the early 1930's. It gained momentum during World War II, when American servicemen unloaded huge amounts of cargo on this and other islands of Melanesia. The cultists believe that the "spiritual" leader who gave the movement its name—John "from" America—will return some day and shower great wealth upon them, where-upon they can quit gardening, kill their pigs, and run (the few) remaining white people off the island.

The colonial masters did not take kindly to the new religion at first, and they imprisoned its leaders—but the John Frum movement managed to survive. Now, with more than half the population of the island as believers, it is accepted as a fact of life on Tanna. The John Frum religion has progressed from *cult* to *culture.*

Prophets and myth-dreams, strange and exotic rituals, and a vision of a hoped-for future....

A small wooden model airplane marks the entrance to Pierre's village which is itself enclosed in a "stockade" of crude wooden posts. The "military" feel to it is conspicuously out of place among the cluster of grass huts beside the roaring sea. Tall flagpoles grace the open space in the centre of the compound. They display not the flag of Vanuatu, but the Stars and Stripes, alongside the insignia of the US Marines, and an independence flag. The cultists ceremoniously hoist the flags each daybreak and lower them again at dusk.

The "headquarters" is at one end of the village. It is of thatch construction containing a number of "administrative" and "military" items: uniforms sporting a "U.S. Marines" label; "rifles" made of bamboo poles, the ends of which have sharp-pointed "bayonettes" painted in bright red; a "map of the globe" (an inflated beach ball) suspended from a pole in the ceiling; and a "bulletin board" displaying information about the operation and history of the movement. "Gospel arrived and missionary stopped our custom not to be exist," reads one of the bulletins. "John Frum Chiefs went to jail for 17 years and today both custom and gospel are now exist on Tanna." At the far end of the village is the "church", a thatch structure housing a large red cross, the symbol of the cult, borrowed from the insignia worn by Red Cross workers who visited the island during the war.

Pierre tells me all about the movement in his fluent French as we wander through the village. The John Frum Movement is commonplace to him; he shows not a hint of skepticism about any of it. To me it seems so bizarre, so far-fetched, so...removed from reality, so unlike anything in the "civilized" world...

Until I stop to think about it. Then I realize a cargo cult is a lot like a western style political party.

In the case of the cargo cult, the doctrine and the "myth-dream" indicate what it is they want, provide an explanation for why they have not received it, and come up with a prescription for how they can get it. The prophet says he knows how others get the cargo and that he can lead them to it. Only at some future point is his explanation found to be faulty. This explains why the prophets have a relatively short period of leadership: simply put, they fail to deliver the goods.

A cargo cult is a lot like a western style political party.

In the case of the western style political party, the policy and principles indicate what it is they want, provide an explanation for why they have not received it, and come up with a prescription for how they can get it. The politician says s/he knows how others "get the cargo" and that s/he can lead them to it. Only at some future point is the explanation found to be faulty. This explains why politicians also have a relatively short period of leadership: simply put, they fail to deliver the goods.

More than that, the problem is, of course, that neither the well-meaning politicians nor their supporters are aware of how the world works outside their political boundaries. The solutions they dream up simply miss the mark, not because they're based on faulty policies or principles but rather, because they do not realize how powerful are the wealthy corporate elites inside their countries.

Some years back in Canada, for example, a standing parliamentary committee on the environment undertook a very serious and very expensive study of global warming. They agreed unanimously that global warming posed a serious threat to Canada, second only to all-out nuclear war. As a result, they recommended a 20 per cent reduction in greenhouse gas emissions by the year 2005.

Of course, nothing was done about it—until five years later when Canada formally committed itself to stabilizing greenhouse gas emissions at the much higher 1990 levels by the year 2000. Reports now indicate that existing federal policies will cause a 13 per cent *rise* from 1990 levels by the year 2000. So who is running the country? Obviously not the politicians! It would seem to be the oil companies, the automobile manufacturers, the bankers...in short, the corporate elite.

Democratic elections might change the party in power every so many years, but that doesn't change the agenda. It is not surprising given the political economy of the western world, not to mention the fact that supposedly opposing parties are really very much alike. Take the case of Canada again. Here are some quotes from party pamphlets. "The Liberal Party is committed to protection of the rights of the individual"; "The Progressive Conservative Party emphasizes the importance of the individual"; "A Liberal government will foster growth and cut the deficit"; the P-C's will "control government spending and reduce the deficit".

From time to time, new parties—like new cargo cults—come on board. They also commit themselves to the rights of the individual, and propose to reduce government spending, cut the deficit, balance the budget, protect the environment, enhance the rights of women and minorities, make government more responsive to the electorate, eliminate patronage, reform the tax system, reduce unemployment, safeguard health care and social programs, reduce family violence, provide childcare, protect cultural heritage.... Once again, hopeful party supporters will fall in line.

Prophets and myth-dreams, strange and exotic rituals, and a vision of a hoped-for future—a future that includes the superior standard of living they see others enjoying while they themselves suffer economic and social powerlessness. It's all a part of culture.

"Names of villages or islands are sometimes placed on the blacklist.
Vakambua, Chief of Mba, thus doomed Tavua, and gave a whale's tooth to the Nggara Chief, that he might, at a fitting time, punish that place. Years passed away, and a reconciliation took place between Mba and Tavua. Unhappily the Mba Chief failed to neutralize the engagement made with Nggara. A day came when human bodies were wanted, and the thoughts of those who held the tooth were turned towards Tavua. They invited the people of that place to a friendly exchange of food, and slew twenty-three of their unsuspecting victims. When the treacherous Nggarans had gratified their own appetites by pieces of the flesh cut off and roasted on the spot, the bodies were taken to Vakambua, who was greatly astonished, expressed much regret that such a slaughter should have grown out of his carelessness, and then shared the bodies to be eaten."

—Rev. Thomas Williams

Recipe # 17
IT MAKES THE BLOOD BOIL

**From CALL as in calling (an ability or vocation)
To PROTOCOL (ceremony and etiquette observed by diplomats)**

In the spring of 1970 I am on my first trip to Asia, pursuing my curiosity about Eastern thought and its application to the so-called "whole mind" approach that balances the left and right sides of the brain. I want to explore the argument that the Western mind is analytical, and leans toward logic and linear thinking, while the Eastern mind is holographic, more attuned to intuition and synchronicity. If one could marry the two hemispheres of the brain, one would be able to realize one's own power, develop vision, and be a positive influence in the world.

That idea is from the *Tao Te Ching* which explores a power that is latent in every individual. According to Lao Tzu, a great Taoist thinker 500 years before the birth of Jesus, this power emerges when one is aware of and aligned with the forces of nature. Lao Tzu taught that an awareness of the patterns of nature would provide insights into parallel patterns in culture. Just as spring follows winter in nature, so does liberation follow domination in culture.

On this particular day I am at the airport in Hong Kong, waiting to board a Japan Airlines flight to Bangkok. It is here I notice a young girl standing off by herself, isolated from the throngs that mill about. She must be in her early twenties but she looks very much a teen-ager—perhaps because she has parted her mid-length hair in twin ponytails and tied them up with brightly-coloured ribbons.

She seems so alone. I walk over and speak to her and we engage in conversation. Nothing of substance. I learn she is a student at MIT, the Massachusetts Institute of Technology. She lives in Bangkok and she is going home for the summer break. She seems very self-assured for someone who has no particular ideas about anything—which surprises me because she is studying at such a prestigious institution.

"What will you do at home for the summer?" I ask her.

She indicates something to the effect that she will just sort of be there and maybe do some things with her father.

"Like, in his business?" I probe.

She gives me a blank stare, which doesn't make sense to me—until later. Our conversation ends and I return to my thoughts on the *Tao Te Ching*.

Just as spring follows winter in nature, so does liberation follow domination in culture.

People who are in alignment with the Tao would be powerful individuals who would never show their strength. They wouldn't need to because others would gravitate toward them. They would radiate knowledge, an intuitive knowing that comes from a direct understanding and experience of nature—they would just *know*. This would be true leadership in society, not pseudo-leadership with its pretentious ceremony and etiquette based on rank. In Lao Tzu's mind, true leadership is founded on intellectual independence—a state of mind in which we have complete trust in our own perceptions and can respond to our own intuition. True power for him is the ability to influence and change the world while living a simple, intelligent, and experientially rich existence.

The passengers board and we jet our way to Thailand. After the heat and humidity of Hong Kong, the comfort of air-conditioning is a welcome relief. It is especially appreciated because every seat on the aircraft is filled. Apart from that, it's a fairly uneventful journey—until we arrive.

The jet touches down on the airstrip and I can see the terminal building in the distance—but we don't taxi there. Instead, the Boeing 707 moves toward a far section of the tarmac. There is no announcement, no explanation.

Eventually we come to a spot where some people have gathered. There is a marching band and a troupe of little girls in brown uniforms. Then I notice, standing in a prominent position, a man dressed in regal attire beside a woman in a white dress with matching white umbrella shading her from the sun: the King and Queen of Thailand.

The jet comes to a full stop. The engines drone to a halt, and with the engines goes the air-conditioning. It is soon very hot and humid; passengers sigh and gasp. There is still no announcement. It's enough to make your blood boil!

I look out the window again. Four men in blue overalls roll out a red carpet. The band strikes up a light marching tune. Moments later, from the forward door of the aircraft emerges the young student from MIT! Now I understand the blank stare. She smiles and responds to the cheers of the crowd as she descends the stairs and walks up the red carpet to her waiting parents, stopping along the way to accept flowers from the little girls in brown uniforms. The princess has returned to her native soil.

People who are in alignment with the Tao would be powerful individuals who would never show their strength.

There are greetings, there are speeches, there are numbers from the band.... I recall the words of Lao Tzu:

Evolved individuals hold to the Tao,
And regard the world as their pattern

Inside the aircraft, the heat is becoming unbearable.

They do not display themselves;
Therefore they are illuminated.

More numbers from the band.

They do not define themselves;
Therefore they are distinguished.

Three-quarters of an hour later, the entourage finally leaves.

They do not make claims;
Therefore they are credited.

The men in blue overalls roll up the red carpet. The engines start and we taxi to the terminal building. There is not enough time, though, to cool the passengers from sweltering heat, sultry humidity—and downright annoyance.

They do not boast;
Therefore they advance.

Yes, the best leadership is unseen; the worst leadership is only to be seen. We have a long way to go—East *and* West.

"*Human bodies are sometimes eaten in connexion with the building of a temple or canoe; or on launching a large canoe; or on taking down the mast of one which has brought some Chief on a visit; or for the feasting of such as take tribute to a principal place.*"

—Rev. Thomas Williams

Recipe # 18
BASTING THEM IN THEIR OWN JUICES

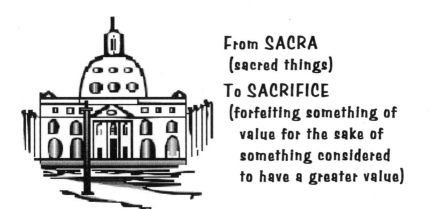

From SACRA
(sacred things)
To SACRIFICE
(forfeiting something of
value for the sake of
something considered
to have a greater value)

It's 1993; there's been a fair bit of coverage on television the past while about a cult in Waco, Texas. Seems some guy there thinks he's Jesus Christ and has managed to convince his followers to believe likewise. As a result, he has some kind of mysterious hold on them. He calls the shots—literally—and they just as literally fall in line. Must be some kind of whacko!

Reminds me of another cult thing a while back. Some guy from India calling himself the Rajneesh managed to get a bunch of people to set him up pretty good somewhere in Oregon. It was no small potatoes. The devotees worked their butts off for this self-styled guru and the wealth poured in. He even managed to acquire a few Rolls Royces. People living near the religious compound were aghast: how could these devotees be taken in like that. Must be some kind of whacko!

But wait a minute! We brought a guy over here from Italy not too many years ago and sent him on an all-expenses-paid trip across Canada. We chartered a jetliner and a few helicopters—gave him the red carpet treatment. It set us back a few million, and he got better than a Rolls; we made special vehicles for him: "pope-mobiles" they called them. TV cameras were on hand to cover it all—and at the end of the tour, there on the tarmac with the cameras still rolling, some big cheese from the publicly-funded CBC television network presented him with a big stack of tapes of all the coverage, for his...electronic photo album, I guess.

I do a bit of "research" and find out this guy is living pretty good back in Italy, too. On a trip to Rome, I tour the Vatican. Pretty spacious digs for a bachelor—and some pricey art to boot! Didn't this guy take a vow of poverty?

I'm looking at all this, and two questions pop into my head. First: if Jesus were alive today, could he get an audience with the Pope? Second: would he want one!

Well, I do—get an audience, that is. Not a private one, mind you. It just happens that I meet a young American traveller whose aunt is a nun at the Vatican. This nun gets some passes, her niece gives me one, and before I know it, I'm having an audience with the Pope.

Pretty spacious digs for a bachelor—and some pricey art to boot! Didn't this guy take a vow of poverty?

There are a few hundred of us in the room—and these people really think this guy is God on earth! They would do just about anything for him, but not for anyone else in the room, I surmise—or even for themselves! They've got it that this guy in a long white robe is somehow of more value than they are. They voluntarily surrender their own spiritual essence and then try to relocate it in him. It's some kind of whacko!

They're not the only ones, of course. We do this with people in a variety of "religious" roles. For example, we call ordained people by titles like "Reverend" or "Father" and make sure we don't swear in front of them. Amazing! A young woman educated in a Catholic school told me she once sought out an archbishop when she had a serious problem. She poured out her soul and at the end of it all, what did he do? How did he respond in her hour of need? He said to her, "You may kiss my ring." Luckily for her, she was speechless, and unable to offer the obvious rejoinder.

Well, anyway, we're at this audience with the Pope and these people have their eyes glued to this solitary figure. I bet most of them don't even see the person sitting next to them where there's probably just as much spiritual growth to be gleaned as they could ever get from this man. That is certainly the case for me. I am sitting beside a young girl from Australia, travelling through Europe with a young man from Kapuskasing, Ontario. After the "audience", we stay together for a time and then say good-bye to each other in the Sistine Chapel. There is something really lovely about this brief encounter. Before we part, we quickly exchange addresses and, right there on the spot, pledge to meet again, somewhere, sometime.

Two questions pop into my head. First: if Jesus were alive today, could he get an audience with the Pope? Second: would he want one!

A few years later I travel to Australia. I remember the pledge in Rome, but I cannot recall what the young girl looks like. From Sydney, I telephone the number she gave me. Remarkably, she is there, living on a homestead with her parents in the Blue Mountains. She instructs me to get on a certain train heading into the interior of the country and after an approximate number of minutes from a certain point I will be at the station closest to where they live. The train doesn't actually stop at these little stations, she tells me, but it will slow down enough so that I can jump off. There is no name to this place, as such, so I won't know when I get there— but she will be standing on the platform and will shout my name. When I hear it, I am to shout hers.

I get on the train and head into the Blue Mountains. It is spectacular countryside. The train puffs its way up the mountains, slowing down now and then at small station crossings. Then, at the approximate time, we approach a platform. I see a young woman standing there, and as the train nears, I hear my name. I shout her name back, we make eye contact, and she hollers, "Jump!"

She lives in a small and very simple dwelling, with the interior of the shelter not yet partitioned. It is August so the temperature is very cool and, at night, I huddle under thick homemade quilts. I have a glorious time, wandering the trails, riding horseback and watching the kangaroos jumping in the "bush". I love it—every bit of it! Even when I am awakened at 3 o'clock one morning by her mother who is standing beside my bed with a long-barreled gun. "Can you shoot a rifle?" she wants to know. Seems the dingoes are killing the sheep.

There is so much to experience in our moment to moment existence if we do not forfeit it for something we think has greater value—if we don't turn *sacra* into *sacrifice*.... The problem is we confuse being spiritual with institutionalized religion. To be spiritual is to be sensitive to life—so sensitive that what we say would be equal to what we do. This would spell an end to organized religion because we would no longer have need of it—and spiritual people would not subscribe to it in any case.

There have been a few figures along the way who have tried to point this out: the Buddha, Jesus, Mohammed, Ramakrishna, Krishnamurti—but we don't get it at the level they're saying it. We turn their messages into dogma and rituals and end up with organized religion. We confuse the map for the territory.

There's a lovely line in a Woody Allen film where a character says, "If Jesus were to come back today, he would never stop throwing up."

We're not as different from that cult in Waco, Texas as we might like to think.

"Cannibalism does not confine its selection to one sex, or a particular age. I have seen the grey-headed and children of both sexes devoted to the oven."

—Rev. Thomas Williams

Recipe # 19
FRYING THEIR BRAINS

From ROUTE
(a course or way)
To ROUTINE
(mechanically performed activities)

It is the *malawa ni mataka*, the Fijian phrase for "daybreak", that brief moment when the sun rises over the black waters of the Pacific transforming the ocean into a deep crystal blue.

Magnificent! Waves breaking softly on the sand. Parrots squawking in the coconut trees. It's a brand new day, a day of infinite possibility in this most perfectly natural setting.

However, it will be like every other day, except Sunday, which will be like every other Sunday. The villagers will automatically rise from their sleeping mats and shift into a full day of "habitual ritual".

Not me. Today Tau and I are taking an excursion to a waterfall on the far side of the island. I want to see this place I've heard about that appears not yet to have been touched by human culture.

The "habitual ritual" we will leave behind is not those activities connected with the production and reproduction of material life. People everywhere need to secure food and shelter and some other things, and it's good to have a "route" to follow, a kind of blueprint for survival. Otherwise, every generation would have to start from scratch, learning how to build a thatch hut, plant a yam garden, organize circle fishing....

No, I'm talking about actions they mechanically perform that have nothing to do with the blueprint. Things they do habitually without critical thought or variation because "it's the custom"—all that "grammatically correct" behaviour that turns *route* into *routine*, that dulls the mind and kills the spirit of adventure.

Habitual ritual is the cultural double-speak that dictates what you must do and what you must not do—or people will rat on you.

We set out early in the morning and walk with the village children as far as the school compound. They are so alive! The little girls are in yellow dresses, strolling quietly on the gravel road and smiling the whole time. The little boys are running up and down the embankment, sliding in the dirt. They would arrive at school looking absolutely filthy but for the fact that the colour of their uniforms is precisely that of the reddish brown soil. I suspect this to be no coincidence.

It's good to have a "route" to follow, a kind of blueprint for survival. Otherwise, every generation would have to start from scratch.

We leave the children at the school compound where they will spend the better part of this spectacular day sitting in a classroom staring at a blackboard. I would like to "rescue" them and take them on this adventure with me. Not to deprive them of education—children are entitled to that—but there's precious little education going on here. Somewhere along the way it seems to have been forgotten that the verb *educate* means "to lead out", that to educate is to create an environment where critical thinking can take place. It's not about *what* to think but about *how* to think. If these Fijian children were really being educated, they would be learning how to step out and look in on their habit systems and their belief systems and see them for what they are. They would be reminded that life is a joyful play of consciousness.

However, that's not what's in store for them today. They're going to get some more training in habitual ritual, learning how to perform activities mechanically without giving them any critical thought. For one thing, their curriculum is an imported one, with much of the instruction in English. They learn by rote and reproduce the correct responses, even though they don't always know what the answers mean. Moreover, they can often provide the correct answers only if the questions are asked in order. In a review exercise, I once skipped from question four to question six; they gave me the answer to question five....

> *Habitual ritual is the cultural double-speak that dictates what you must do and what you must not do.*

Furthermore, it doesn't help matters that their textbooks are out of date. Here's something from an English grammar exercise: "One of the most important (woman, women) in the world is Mrs. Gandhi." Even the right answer is wrong. Of course, the whole point is to make them "grammatically correct". Frying their brains....

Beyond the school, we get a lift with a passing lorry that takes us to the end of the road. From here it's on foot along jungle paths and stretches of beach. We see no one, apart from a few women from a far village diving for shellfish.

We stop to drink some coconut water, then continue along the beach until we come to a *galala* ("free") homestead which belongs to a family related to Tau. They have opted to live independently of the communal village system. How refreshing, I think, to find someone who has broken away from all that habitual ritual!

We share a late morning meal with them. They are cooking fish, but according to custom, cannot serve it to us because Tau belongs to a clan that is *kai-wai*—literally, "people of the water"; in other words, fishers. His cousins here belong to the *kai-vanua*, "people of the land", or farmers. It is taboo for *kai-vanua* to serve fish to *kai-wai*. (Where is it written?) Habitual ritual! The taboo doesn't apply to crustaceans, however, so they serve us crayfish cooked in coconut milk—which is okay by me.

We continue our journey. From this point on, the scenery

is spectacular, like a set from a Tarzan movie. At times, we pull our way through thick jungle by clinging to leaves and vines. Sometime after midday—I have no record of the time—we reach our destination, and the space in which I now find myself is like a mythological Garden of Eden. A fresh water river winds through the jungle, spilling over rocks on its way to the sea. The flowing stream is banked on one side by deep rock walls dripping with moisture, on the other by thick dense foliage. The scene is breathtaking. It appears as though no human being has ever been here. Not a tree, not a leaf, not a vine has been disturbed. There is something primordial about it, and it seems possible in this instance to exist again (or for the very first time) in a pure state of innocence—without social systems, or belief systems, or "knowledge of good and evil". We take off our clothes and jump into the water.

It's so pure, so translucent. In every direction I see natural contours, glistening shapes, deep shadows. Everything is creative, like nature giving birth to itself. Then there's Tau with his tall, brown body, slim waist and muscles toned to perfection. A genuine warmth emulates from his smiling lips and deep brown eyes. I see him now not as clansman or fisherman, not as Fijian or Melanesian, not in any of his roles or ranks or categories. He is life grown conscious of itself, the perfect completion to this natural environment. Time is suspended....

Everything is creative, like nature giving birth to itself.

I know it can't last forever. I know we must return to a place where people live and move and "have their being" within a maze of mechanically performed activities....

It's a long silent walk back to the village. We arrive just in time for the prescribed evening prayers—the same words, the same gestures....

From the natural to the cultural, from the primordial to the ideological, from the spontaneous to the mechanical...life ceases to be a joyful play of consciousness.

It's easy to see all this in the Fijian village, but it's not just the Fijians who've "got the habit". When I stop to think about it, I realize there's plenty of habitual ritual where I come from too. For example, in just about any North American household I know, the family members always sit at the same place around the dinner table. Why?

People always sleep on the same side of the bed! Amazing! We have a library of cookbooks but continue to prepare the same ten recipes. When we go out to dine, we go to the same restaurants, even order the same dishes. We keep returning to the same holiday destination, where we stay in the same accommodation....

Habitual ritual—that dulls the mind and kills the spirit of adventure.

From the natural to the cultural...life ceases to be a joyful play of consciousness.

We lock ourselves into jobs we don't like in order to support a life-style that leads to boredom and discontent. When we get time off on weekends, what do we do? For one thing, we mow the lawn—not because we like mowing lawns, but if you don't, the neighbours will "rat" on you.

All that grammatically correct "How do you do?"—(how do you do what?)—reveals just how afraid we are to think contrary to the established patterns of society, and just how willing we are to be falsely respectful of authority and tradition.

Is this the grand design for the human race? Was it intended to be a rat race? There's a funny thing about that analogy. People talk about "the rat race" as a metaphor for frenzy. Well, the interesting thing about rats is that if you run them through a maze with four tunnels and put cheese at the end of only one, the rats will explore all the tunnels until they find the cheese, and they'll remember where the cheese is. Repeat it, and they'll head straight for the right tunnel every time. If you switch the cheese to a different tunnel, they'll continue down the old one until they discover the cheese is no longer there. Then they'll switch and search again until they find the new tunnel—and they'll stay with the new one only so long as it continues to deliver the cheese.

The difference between people and rats is that people will keep heading down the same old tunnel even though the cheese is no longer there.

Them rats might not be "grammatically correct", but they sure is usin' them's brains. How come them's humans isn't? 'Cause them's brains is fried!

The difference between people and rats is that people will keep heading down the same old tunnel even though the cheese is no longer there.

Ni dromu na siga, Fijian for "sunset". They light up the kerosene lamps and gather to drink kava. The same words, the same gestures. They pick up their ukuleles and start to sing. The same lyrics, the same rhythms....

Oh well.... I reach for my guitar.

"Ovens and pots in which human flesh is cooked, and dishes or forks used in eating it, are strictly tabu for any other purpose."

—Rev. Thomas Williams

Recipe # 20
FROM THE FRYING PAN INTO THE FIRE

From SOURCE
(a point of origin)
To SORCERY
(black magic)

You would think they'd be the healthiest people in the world. They have fresh unpolluted air and natural sunshine, clear sparkling water, papayas and mangoes and pineapples, taro and breadfruit and yams, mineral-rich seaweed, and a reef full of fresh fish....

Yet the Fijians get sick early and die young. Since the arrival of the Europeans, they have passed up life-giving fruits and vegetables in favour of imported white flour, sugar, salt, tea and tobacco. These deadly foods, added to an already high acid diet of fish and yams, eaten together at the same meal, constitute a recipe for disaster—and disaster strikes often.

Since the arrival of the Europeans, they have passed up life-giving fruits and vegetables in favour of imported white flour, sugar, salt, tea and tobacco.

It's Monday, early in April, the week before Easter. Tiwa,

a woman in our village, is sick. She has been lying down for a number of days now and Saki, her husband, has arranged for her to stay with Nana, a folk healer in the neighbouring village. This morning I go with the women from Tiwa's clan to Nana's village to visit Tiwa. The women bring gifts.

We gather inside Nana's *bure* (thatched hut). Tiwa is asleep and Nana says it is the first time she has slept since she arrived three days earlier so we don't wake her. We make our presentations and then the wife of the local Methodist church leader speaks about the love of God. This is followed by a series of prayers from the women.

Tiwa is lying down on a mat under a mosquito net. She is a very large woman in her early forties, sick from lack of exercise and an improper diet consisting of too much white flour, sugar, salt, tea and tobacco. Now she is surrounded by a group of kinswomen who show their concern by praying and bringing her gifts of white flour, sugar, salt, tea and tobacco.

These deadly foods...constitute a recipe for disaster—and disaster strikes often.

On Tuesday Tiwa is still sick and her family takes further means to protect her. They think there is some kind of sorcery being done and the most likely origin of it, in their minds, is the big tree outside the family *bure*. It has large sprawling limbs and thick green leaves. Today, to counter the sorcery, they cut down the tree—which is really unfortunate because it's the only tree in the area and the family often used to sit beneath its wide shady branches to avoid the heat of the day. Tonight, all the branches lay on the ground and only the bare stump remains. Also, last night one of the older ladies in the village told Tiwa's daughter not to leave any clothes on the line overnight as whoever is doing the sorcery might use one of the articles to work their black magic. Tonight the chief, the village elders and the men from the sick woman's clan gather inside her house to make an offering of kava in an attempt to reverse what they suspect is going on. Through all this, Tiwa remains in the next village with Nana, who by now has had to borrow money from her son to feed the patient and all the visitors who are coming to see her.

Wednesday. Tiwa is taken to the island's nursing station. The attendant who sees her there says she has "sugar disease and salt disease". They will send her to the medical station further up the coast today so a doctor can examine her and make arrangements, if necessary, to send her to the hospital in Suva, on the main island. However, the nurse expresses concern that it may already be too late to help her.

Thursday, the day before Good Friday. A large number of villagers go circle fishing after breakfast for tomorrow's feasting. They go as far as the reef and arrive back with a huge catch of fish in late afternoon. About 5 o'clock the lorry returns from the other side of the island. Instead of parking in its usual spot at the end of the pathway into the village, it comes right across the village green. Then I see Saki step from the front seat and go over to where the women are cleaning fish. Immediately the women start crying really loudly, so I know that Tiwa has died. They have brought her body back in the lorry with them.

Immediately all the Easter plans are given over to death ceremonies. They take Tiwa's body to a sleeping house where the older women prepare it for viewing. They place the body on three nicely decorated mats at the upper end of the house. Then they cover it with tapa cloth. While this is going on, the men hastily construct a palm frond shelter outside the house; this is where the funeral delegations will be received and where the exchange ceremonies will take place. They set up a second shelter of palm fronds beside the house of the chief of the clan; this is where the communal cooking and eating will take place.

Within the context of the culture, the most appropriate contribution I can make is...a bag of flour. This I do with more than slight trepidation, because the only flour I can get is processed white, which I know will contribute to the very thing that has taken Tiwa's life. I also know they are going to consume at least one full bag of the stuff in any case and they will struggle to find the $30 to pay for it if I don't—so a bag of flour it will be.

The mourning rituals for Tiwa are very different from those held for the chief of Nana's village who died two weeks ago.

When the chief died, no one was allowed to cry; now every-one is supposed to. Once again, they do it collectively; they start and stop on cue. Each time a new delegation of women arrives in the "house of death", they first go forward to view the body. Some hug the corpse, others lay their heads on it for a brief time. Then they begin crying loudly. When a close relative arrives, the wailing takes on heightened intensity and gets very high-pitched. Then just as suddenly as it started, it stops.

I stay in the "house of death" until about 2 o'clock in the morning. Then I go over to where the women are baking huge pans of bread, buns, scones and pancakes. All this processed white flour is going into the bodies of these people tomorrow morning while they prepare to bury one of their kin who died from more of the same.

When a close relative arrives, the wailing takes on heightened intensity and gets very high-pitched. Then just as suddenly as it started, it stops.

Tiwa's funeral is held on Good Friday. The lay preacher says she died from "sugar disease and salt disease—and sor-cery". From the frying pan into the fire....

The story might have had a different ending if they had more knowledge about vitamins and minerals, and food com-bining; if they knew about the ill effects of white flour, sugar, salt, tea and tobacco, and the dangers of eating fried foods; if they knew the positive benefits of regular exercise; if they had a health care system readily accessible to all....

In Canada, we have all those things. So you'd think we Canadians would be the healthiest people in the world. Far from it. We pollute our drinking water and the air we breathe. We add chemicals and preservatives to our food, and put sugar and salt in just about everything. We inject growth hormones into cows and chickens and then eat their car-casses. We pour dioxins, heptachlors, PCB's and other hy-drocarbons into our lakes and streams where they con-centrate in the fish we eat. We mix fish—along with other animal carcasses—into cattle feed to make up for protein deficiencies caused by forced-growth hormones, so we get the pollutants again, concentrated in our meat and dairy products. We feast on food that is fast and fried instead of fresh and alive, then wash it all down with huge quantities of beer and soft drinks, laced with sugar and artificial sweeteners. Autointoxication: the poisoning of the body by toxic matters generated therein.

When the body breaks down from the toxic overload, off we run to the sick-care system to get a dose of prescription drugs. From the frying pan into the fire! And when the drugs can no longer hold back the floodgates, we remove the offending organs and glands. Out come tonsils, adenoids, appendix, gall bladder, uterus, breasts, prostate, portions of the stomach, liver, lungs, intestines...as though the human body comes equipped with spare parts!

When the drugs can no longer hold back the floodgates, we remove the offending organs and glands.

"Coke. It's the real thing." "Pepsi, the choice of a new generation." And, "What you want is what you get at McDonalds."

From *source...*

"Just one calorie. Diet Coke."

...to *sorcery.*

"Two all beef patties, special sauce, lettuce, cheese, pickles, onions on a sesame seed bun."

From the frying pan...

"You've got the right one, baby."

...into the fire.

"Uh-huh."

"Bodies...are often mutilated in a frightful manner, a treatment which is considered neither mean nor brutal."
—Rev. Thomas Williams

Recipe # 21

SPARE RIBS

From PETITION
(a solemn request)

To COMPETITION
(vying with others for profit or position)

Vanuatu's remote location in the southwestern Pacific gives it an image of mystery and romance. With its pleasant climate and fertile soil it is a true tropical paradise. Here, far off the beaten track, people are still living in a tribal system that has remained unchanged for centuries. They call it their "custom" way of life. Right now I'm in one of these stone age "custom villages" on the island of Tanna.

It is very "primitive". Women and girls wear only a grass skirt which extends from the waist to the ankle. Men and boys (once they have been circumcised) wear only a penis sheath. They garden with digging sticks and hunt with bows and arrows. They cook and sleep in crude grass huts, the only "western" objects in their possession being steel axes and iron cooking pots. The pots are never washed, by the way; they are hung from the ceiling in the kitchen huts when not in use to prevent the pigs from licking them.

Tanna is famous for its food festival called *niel* which is actually an alliance ritual between villages. This is how it works: one village (which is really a big clan) grows a huge amount of yams and then invites another village to come and take them away. It's done with a lot of pomp and ceremony, feasting and dancing. Moreover, they "acquire" agricultural magic to make the yams grow fast and high and strong. When it comes time to host a *niel*, they select the choice yams, decorate them, and heap them into gigantic piles to show them off to their best advantage. They even hang them from the trees.

Of course, it works two ways. The clan receiving the yams will give back the equivalent of what it has received at some point in the future. Their agricultural magicians will work their own spells to make their yams grow faster, higher, stronger. And when they host a *niel*, they will carry it out with the same pomp and ceremony, feasting and dancing.

Sometimes it takes several years to organize a *niel*. The last one on Tanna was four years ago so it's no small (sweet) potatoes! All this simply to create or maintain an alliance—which is important, because if you look back (and not that far back) into the history of the island, you will discover these same clans used to raid each other's villages, destroying their homes and gardens. And while they were at it, they would engage in a little *netik* (sorcery), killing off a member of the other's kin. Thus was set into motion a cycle of murder and revenge, the Tannese version of warfare. Better just to give the guy your yams than have him burn your house and kill your wife and daughter!

The food festival on Tanna is a sacred event, a solemn request to your neighbours that you be allowed to live your life in peace and prosperity. It makes perfectly good sense, not to mention a very good excuse to go dancing! But that's not the whole story. In spite of its potential "peace dividend" and high entertainment value, the *niel* eventually became subverted to the ambitions of the Melanesian "Big Man".

Better just to give the guy your yams than have him burn your house and kill your wife and daughter!

A "Big Man" is the type of person who combines a small amount of interest in his tribe's welfare with a great deal of self-interested calculation for his own personal gain. The authority he comes to wield is personal. That is to say, he does not hold office nor is he elected. His status is the result of acts which serve to raise him above most other members of his tribe and attract to him a local band of followers. They admire him, give their energy and labour to him, and root for him (literally and figuratively)—but the benefits gained are almost entirely his own.

The opposite of a "Big Man" is a "rubbish man", and it seems one will go to great lengths to achieve the one and avoid the other. A rubbish man sports no outstanding ability, no special skill, no cherished social distinction. It is enough to give one a deep-seated feeling of worthlessness! Paradoxically, the one creates the other. In the process of supporting a Big Man, the local band of followers relinquish their own possibilities for outstanding achievement and end up, more or less, as someone else's "spare ribs".

So, with time, the *niel* has become less a *petition* between villages and more a *competition* between Big Men. The trick for the Big Man, of course, is to keep the corporate sponsorship intact by appearing to bring home the goods for the group at large when, in fact, the village as a whole does not cash in on his profit, prize or position. It's a most peculiar phenomenon! A fascinating aspect of Melanesian culture.

I return to Canada just in time to catch the television coverage of the 1994 Winter Games in Lillehammer, Norway. The Olympics, I am reminded, also started out as a sane alternative to local warfare, this time in ancient Greece. Indeed, at the four-year intervals, a sacred truce was declared and enforced to allow athletes to travel unmolested to and from the Games. The Games themselves were sacred and the greatest honour then to be attained by any Greek was the winning of the simple olive branch—a symbol of peace— given to the victor. But winning wasn't everything. The gracefulness and sportsmanship of the contestant and the method of winning were esteemed equally with the victory itself.

These great Olympians became heroes. Their feats of skill and courage were recorded by poets and writers of the time while sculptors preserved their strength and beauty in marble. They symbolized that optimal blend of toned body and developed mind, of robust health and moral character, of physical activity and artistic expression.

They were amateurs in the true sense of the word. "Amateur" didn't mean "not-yet-professional"; it meant one who participated in a sport as an avocation without material gain of any kind. Indeed, one could not even qualify if he had not ensured his livelihood by other means or if he currently or even previously received remuneration for participation in the sport.

They symbolized that optimal blend of toned body and developed mind, of robust health and moral character, of physical activity and artistic expression.

Like the festival on Tanna, the modern Olympics has succumbed to the ambitions of the "Big Man". The amateurs I'm watching (live by satellite) are full-time professional "big men" performing the most amazing feats of skill and courage, if not downright recklessness. "Oh, what an excellent start: two one-hundredths of a second faster than the first run!" shouts the commentator. They race down mountainsides at breakneck speeds; collapse, exhausted, at the end of cross-country ski trails; elbow their way to medals in short track speed skating.... "Faster, higher, stronger": they risk it all, not for the olive branch, and not for country, but for pieces of silver and gold.

And I mean silver and gold, because these professional athletes cash in big! "Did you ever imagine it would come to this?" the commentator asks one of the victors. "Not in my wildest imagination," comes the reply as we are shown her picture on the front of a box of processed breakfast cereal. She has won medals before, but she's "tasting them again for the very first time". Another Olympian, in her search for gold, "eats plenty of chicken noodle soup".

As in Melanesia, the victory only appears to belong to the group at large. "Wake up, Canada," the commentator announces first thing in the morning, "You have won a gold medal!" Well, wake up, commentator! The medal is not *for* Canada, it's *from* Canada. *From* Russia. *From* Norway. From the "local bands of followers", the "spare ribs", who admire, support, root for and cheer, while benefits go to the victors in the form of lucrative endorsements for fast foods, soft drinks and chocolate bars, products that hardly qualify as having contributed to their athletic prowess. The sacred games have become profane business, a first rate marketing tool for pushing all manner of consumer products, and the athletes quickly learn to measure their medals in hard cash.

They risk it all, not for the olive branch, and not for country, but for pieces of silver and gold.

"Share the spirit!" That's the motto—but the Olympic *spirit* has turned into Olympic *fever* as the daily medal count vicariously bolsters national pride. The victors stand beneath their national flags (symbols of war, by the way) while the anthems play. Ironically, they reminisce about Sarajevo, a former site of the Winter Games where the Olympic flame has been replaced by fire of another kind. The irony is reinforced by an athlete who unwittingly skates her program as a tribute to the war-torn city by gliding and twirling over the ice to the music of "Where Have all the Flowers Gone?".

Gone to graveyards, every one....

When will they ever learn?

The song is more a metaphor than a tribute. The athletes talk about "smelling blood", "killing" the opposing team, "fighting to the finish", and "battling for the Bronze". Sounds like life on Tanna before the sacred food festival! And life in ancient Greece before the sacred Games! "Once in awhile we get a glimpse of what life could be," states one of the sponsors, "when the Olympic Games bring people together in peace and harmony, and the dream that one day this is what life will be like."

I hope not! And my thoughts are shared by a good number of the athletes themselves who still cling to the Olympic ideal. "It's just sport; it's supposed to be *fun*," cries a downhill racer. "but it's got extreme." "I need to reevaluate," states another, "I need to find out what is real." Not all of them keep it in check, however. One magazine quotes an athlete-in-training as saying, "My muscles are very tired but the more I suffer now, the less I will suffer at the Olympics."

The sacred games have become profane business, a first rate marketing tool for pushing all manner of consumer products, and the athletes quickly learn to measure their medals in hard cash.

It's better than all-out war, of course, for the scene rarely gets violent, although once in awhile someone does get whacked across the knees to put them out of competition. Even at its best, however, there is an undercurrent of pathos when *petition* is turned to *competition*. Take the case of the young orphan girl from the Ukraine who becomes "Queen of the Ice" with her stunning gold medal performance. Does she beam with triumph? No. She clings desperately to her coach and cries—and they are not tears of joy. I see a catharsis from deep-seated grief—for a father missing and presumed dead, for grandparents who were victims of Chernobyl, for a mother who has recently died of cancer. There is nothing left to petition; she must settle for a piece of lifeless metal.

Then there is the American speed-skater who has only "one last chance for gold, for glory, for good" as the commentator puts it. He *finally* wins his medal—and *everyone* is relieved that his "Olympic ordeal", not to mention that of his wife, is finally over. "How will it change your life?" asks the commentator of the couple. "It will make a great deal of difference in terms of notoriety," the wife replies.

Notoriety?!

There is a lesser known "athlete", a French peasant by the name of Elzeard Bouffier whose solitary life in the mountains of France was recorded in book* and on film as "the man who planted trees".

"I asked him if he owned the land," writes the author. "He said no. Did he know who owned it? He did not. He thought it was common land, parish property, or perhaps it belonged to people who did not care about it. That did not concern him and so, with infinite care, he planted his hundred acorns."

Over time, dense and strong trees stretched as far as the eye could see over what had been previously barren land. "Regular work in a peaceful atmosphere," sums up the author, "brisk mountain air, the simple life and above all peace of mind had endowed this old man with almost awe-inspiring health; he was one of God's athletes."

Elzeard Bouffier reminds me that we cannot be compared, opposed, pitted against one another—even in sport—without simultaneously cultivating the life-force deep within that allows us to feel humility, compassion and love—not just for ourselves but for the whole of life. Until we can safeguard the ethic that gives meaning to life, we can create neither a true champion nor a lasting peace.

We cannot be compared, opposed, pitted against one another—even in sport—without simultaneously cultivating the life-force deep within that allows us to feel humility, compassion and love.

The Olympic Games come to an end. Before the sacred flame can be extinguished, however, many of the victors have already departed from the village. Off they go with their shiny new medals, themselves to become the "spare ribs" of the giant consumer industries. In four years, at an Olympic village on the other side of the world, they will go through the riual all over again.

When will they ever learn....

"*Revenge is undoubtedly the main cause of cannibalism in Fiji, but by no means invariably so. I have known many cases in which such a motive could not have been present. Sometimes, however, this principle is horribly manifested.*"

—Rev. Thomas Williams

Recipe # 22
COLD CUTS

From AGE
(to grow up)

To SAVAGE
(not civilized)

It is January, 1994 and I am trading the cold Canadian winter for the hot humid climate of Western Samoa. It's a small island country, less than three thousand square kilometers of land on two major islands, Upolu and Savaii, with a population of about 170,000 people.

It's very hot this time of year, the middle of summer. On this particular day I head out to the beautiful beach at Lalomanu on the eastern tip of Upolu where there is excellent snorkelling and breath-taking scenery. The driver is a Samoan man, probably in his mid-forties. He wears only a simple wrap-around cloth, a *lavalava*, revealing elaborate tattooing from his rib cage to below his knees. He tells me it is both very painful and very expensive to have the process done.

With us on this excursion is a group of small boys ranging in age from eight to twelve years along with an adult female attendant. The boys are his "children", the driver says, meaning they are part of his *aiga* or extended family. He is taking them to the beach at Lalomanu so they can swim in the ocean because they have just been circumcised and the salt water will help prevent infection.

The boys are visibly uncomfortable despite their constant grinning. They sit in the van, holding their *lavalavas* well away from their pubic areas to alleviate the stinging.

Circumcision goes back a long way in this part of the world. It was and still is a big part of "coming of age in Samoa".

The drive is beautiful, along the southeast coast of Upolu, passing Falefa Falls, across the Le Mafa Pass with its commanding view of the shoreline, through lush green forests, more waterfalls, plantations and traditional Samoan villages dotted along the coastline.

When we arrive at the beach, the young boys throw off their *lavalavas* and run naked into the water. Blood and puss ooze from their swollen but tiny penises. For the next few hours they rollick and swim in the ocean, climb along the trunks of the leaning coconut trees that overhang the beach, and watch me snorkelling. They're having a very good time, despite the obvious discomfort.

Circumcision goes back a long way in this part of the world. It was and still is a big part of "coming of age in Samoa". It's not quite the same as circumcision in the English sense of the word. *Ole tofogo*, from *tofo* meaning "to cut" is a simple cutting of the foreskin. An incision is made in the upper margin by pushing a spatula under the foreskin and cutting it through with a blow from a sharp object such as a shark's tooth, a mussel shell, a piece of slit bamboo, or—as is more common nowadays—a steel knife. After the cutting, the youth is told to run into the salt water.

The painful ritual usually takes place at the onset of puberty, but it can be anytime between seven and fifteen years of age. It would seem to be very important because it is said no self-respecting Samoan girl would sleep with an uncircumcised man.

The circumcised youth has now attained manhood—well, not quite. That's only half of it. To attain manhood *fully*—that is, to be marriageable—there is something more required: tattooing.

An incision is made in the upper margin by pushing a spatula under the foreskin and cutting it through with a blow from a sharp object such as a shark's tooth.

Traditionally, tattooing was the mark of reaching *taia*—manhood—literally, "old enough to be tattooed". Males, almost without exception, subjected themselves to these painful operations as soon as they were of age. The exceptions were considered *pala'ai*, "cowards", "weaklings". Chiefs refused to accept food from them. Indeed, many refused their daughters to marry them. Others turned their backs on the mission schools because students there were forbidden to be tattooed.

Tattooing applied to both sexes: on boys, from the false ribs to below the knees; on girls, almost never beyond the thighs. They both went through the painful ordeal at puberty. For the young and not yet tattooed, there is a special term in Samoan; it is *tamala ta*, literally, "child not tattooed".

Tattooing was done with the *'au*, a needle made of bone, preferably human bone. That it was painful is evident from the song of the *tufuga*, tattoo artist, while tattooing a chief.

A nei fo'i nanei e tilotilo i ou malofie, pei ni lau ti usi e.

(Patience, only a short while, and you will see your tattoo which will resemble the fresh leaf of the ti-plant.)

O a'u lava le alofa atu nei, tapai sau amoga, ta fesuia'i ma lota alofa.

(I feel sorry for you. I wish it were a burden which I could take off your shoulders in love and carry for you.)

'Aue, 'o le toto e, taia ma oso i le tino, taulaga ai le malolo.

(O, the blood! It is springing out of your body at every stroke; try to be strong.)

E isia le'ula, isia le fau, ae le isia si au tatau, a si au 'ula tutumau e te alu ma 'oe i le tu'ugamau.

(Your necklace may break, the fau-tree may burst, but my

tattooing is indestructible.)

Incidentally, there was no song for the tattooing of a common man, or for a woman.

Perhaps these island people have a different idea about pain, especially where vanity and ambition are involved. Otherwise, why would they subject themselves to such painful rituals. Surely life is not meant to be an ordeal. Wouldn't these children "come of age" all by themselves, sort of like the way a kitten naturally turns into a cat?

Perhaps these island people have a different idea about pain, especially where vanity and ambition are involved.

It's so..."primitive", so..."uncivilized", so..."savage". How lucky we are that *we* don't have to go through such torture to "come of age".

Yup. We're lucky all right. Do you remember sitting for long hours on hard wooden seats, arranged in straight rows in box-like rooms, staring at a blackboard and a home room teacher under artificial fluorescent lights? Where you had to put up your hand and ask—in front of the whole class—just to leave the room to go to the bathroom? Where right outside the window—when you dared to look out—you could see the sunlight and you longed to go out and play in it, and by the time they let you out the best part of the day was already gone?

School! Where your movements were choreographed to the sound of the morning bell, the recess bell, the lunch bell...day after week after month after year.... Wouldn't it be better just to get one quick blow with a shark's tooth or a mussel shell or a piece of slit bamboo and then go jump in the ocean? Come to think of it, those Samoan boys got off "real easy"!

Then there was church. More hard benches arranged in more straight rows and more boring lectures. For this one, if you were a young lady you had to wear a hat, not to mention a brassiere, nylon stockings and a dress cut from synthetic fibres. The guys didn't fare much better: tight, buttoned collars; belted suits and choking neckties.

Then it was on to university where the cold winter winds blew drifting snow across the frozen stretches between lecture halls. No matter what the temperature, women were compelled to show their hemlines: freezing ankles, freezing bums.... It was torture!

Wouldn't it be better just to get one quick blow with a shark's tooth...and then go jump in the ocean?

The grammar, the dress code, the diploma: the marks of a "man" and a "woman". "I feel sorry for you," drones the teacher/ clergyman/university lecturer, "I wish it were a burden I could take off your shoulders in love and carry for you." Real tattoo artists!

Just like the Samoans, we are marked for life, wearing high-heeled shoes that pinch the feet and throw out the back, suits and ties that constrain circulation, bras that literally "cross your heart", synthetic materials that won't let the body breathe....

We seem to have an extraordinary ability to withstand pain, especially where vanity and ambition are involved. God forbid that we should "slip into something comfortable" and experience a sense of serenity.

"*The carver was a young man; but he seemed skillful. He used a piece of slit bamboo, with which, after having washed the body in the sea, he cut off the several members, joint by joint.*"

—Rev. Thomas Williams

Recipe # 23
THE FAMILY BARBECUE

From **BOND**
(a cohesion between parts)

To **BONDAGE**
(the condition of a slave)

It is early in my career as an academic and I am a Research Associate with the University of Delhi in India. It is here I come to share accommodation with a young woman who is pursuing a Ph.D. in History. She is a quiet type, well conditioned in the demure attitude and demeanour of the traditional Indian woman and, as a result, I do not get to know her well.

I am studying a cross-cultural development aid program between Canada and India that isn't working. Everything is in place but, for some reason, nothing is happening. Nobody is quite sure why; my role is to get to the bottom of it.

Well, it doesn't take a genius to figure out there is a culture conflict—but it might take one to articulate it, because culture is a very tricky thing to get a handle on. I approach the problem by comparing the way we instill values within the two cultural traditions. What I discover is that the values are not only incompatible; they are opposed!

In Canada, our values spring from a Graeco-Christian heritage. If children reared in this Western tradition begin by taking moral instructions from their parents, it is with the firm expectation that they will mature to question and to make independent decisions on issues which earlier were decided for them. In religious language, it is movement from "honour thy father and thy mother" to "be ye transformed by the renewing of your minds".

The consequence of all this, by the time we mature, is that we make a big deal about rationality. We analyze everything! Moreover, we are never satisfied with what we find, so we continually dream up something new or better. And we don't stop there; we then figure out a way to turn our schemes into reality. It's the old one-two-three punch of Christianity: size up a situation, adopt a course of action, and then "Just do it!". You might say we Christians like to shape our history rather than being shaped by our myths.

It's a different picture on the other side of the globe. In Hindu India, children are not responsible and incur no blame for their actions until they are eight years old. Then they "enter society", where the accent is on proper behaviour and regular habits. Now they must learn the formalities of correct relationships with each member of the family according to rank, and conform to the norms of caste and sub-caste behaviour.

Consequently, adult Hindu Indians have a very different take on things from people in the West. Dr. Sudhir Kakar, a prominent psychoanalyst here in Delhi, says that Hindus are not so interested in changing the outside world. They're much more concerned with "the inner world", and with notions like *moksha* (self-realization), *dharma* (right action), and *karma* (the endless cycle of birth, growth and death). *

We Christians like to shape our history rather than being shaped by our myths.

I meet with Dr. Kakar to discuss my research findings. He concurs that Indian and Western value systems are at odds. In Hindu India, he says, to size up a situation for oneself and to act on one's own judgements is to take an enormous cultural as well as personal risk. For most Hindus, this kind of independent action would be unthinkable.

Here's the way he summarizes it: "With the Hindu emphasis on man's inner limits, there is not that sense of urgency and struggle against the outside world, with prospects of...great achievements just around the corner, that seem to propel Western lives. In any case, given the *totality* of the Hindu world image, such a struggle would be viewed as taking place on the wrong battlefield and fought with the wrong weapons."**

That's a great way to put it!

I return to my accommodation where my young Indian roommate is busy at her desk. We have sizeable and comfortable quarters by Indian standards and just outside the main window is a huge tree gloriously adorned with brilliant red flowers. I gaze at it long and hard.

"What a beautiful tree!" I say to her.

"Where?" she replies.

"Outside the window."

She glances through the window. "Oh," she murmurs, and goes back to her books.

"Did you notice that tree before?" I ask her.

"No," she replies.

Now, this tree is huge and bright red in colour; how could anybody not see it! I get really curious. Does this have anything to do with values or the enculturation process, or is she just so engrossed in her history books that she is not aware of anything going on around her? I ask her, "What made you decide to take a Ph.D. in History?"

"Oh, I didn't decide," she replies. "My parents decided for me."

"Your parents decided that you would take a Ph.D. in History?"

"Yes."

"Well, do you like doing a Ph.D. in History?"

"I guess so. I haven't thought about it."

"Well, just think about it now. If you could do anything you wanted to do, what would it be?"

"I don't know."

"Isn't there anything you would really like to do?"

Silence. Blank stare.

"Just pretend you can choose whatever you want to study or whatever work you want to do. What would it be?"

Protracted silence.

"What do you like doing?"

More silence.

Finally she speaks. "Maybe I would take some kind of secretarial course."

What can I say! It has to be values—the Hindu caste system and all that. Being born into a traditional occupation, conditioned by parents to accept without question. *Moksha ...dharma...karma.....*

Hold on! How many parents in the West do the same thing! How many young Canadians or Americans or Europeans end up becoming doctors or lawyers or accountants because that's what their parents want them to become. That has nothing to do with the *Christian* world view any more than this has to do with the *Hindu* world view. It has to do with the *Family* world view. It's the idea—in the West, in India and all over the world—that parents own their children, or at least are entitled to control their minds. All over the planet, we witness one generation telling the next what to do with their lives....

How many young Canadians or Americans or Europeans end up becoming doctors or lawyers or accountants because that's what their parents want them to become.

And a woman who held a babe against her bosom said,

Speak to us of Children.

And he said:

Your children are not your children.

They are the sons and daughters of Life's longing for itself.

They come through you but not from you,

And though they are with you they belong not to you.

Kahlil Gibran.***

You may give them your love but not your thoughts,

For they have their own thoughts.

You may house their bodies but not their souls,

For their souls dwell in the house of tomorrow,
   which you cannot visit, not even in your dreams.
You may strive to be like them,
   but seek not to make them like you.
For life goes not backward nor tarries with yesterday....

It is true a child needs a little push to get going, and a family is a good starting block—but once you take off and join the human race, you have to be able to run your own course. Don't parents know that? Would they really subject a human being to a life of history books or medical journals or legal texts without even knowing if s/he likes history or medicine or law?

You bet they would! It starts when children are very young with that imposing question: "What do you want to be when you grow up?", as though *being* were not self-evident. It takes the innocence of a Forrest Gump to set us straight. "Want to be?" he replies to that question, "Aren't I going to be *me?*"

Once you take off and join the human race, you have to be able to run your own course.

It's the family barbecue, where *bond* is transformed into *bondage*. We do it so our children will get a better job, and achieve some kind of distinction, and be a more efficient clog in the economic machine, and have wider domination over others.... Never mind that they do not reflect on the significance of life, or develop deep integration of thought and feeling. Never mind that their lives are incomplete, or that they contribute to the misery and suffering of the world.

"*The cannibal fork seems to be used for taking up morsels of the flesh when cooked as a hash, in which form the old people prefer it.*"

—Rev. Thomas Williams

Recipe # 24
GUESS WHO'S GONNA BE DINNER

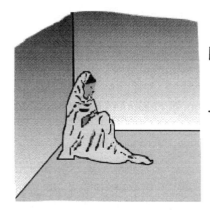

From **PROMISE**
(indication of future
excellence)
To **PROMISCUITY**
(indiscriminate mingling
in sexual matters)

During another visit to New Delhi I find myself more or less adopted into a young Sikh family whose roots are in a small village near the border of the Punjab. While I am here, a man from their village comes to the city—for the first time—to get a replacement part for his tractor. The thing I notice about him is that he always wears a green turban, so I refer to him as *hara pugni valla*, "green turban wearer". The label sticks, so much so that to this day I cannot remember his "real" name.

A few days later, I am invited to take a trip to the village with my host Bhai ("brother") and "Hara Pugni-valla" to attend a wedding. We set out from Delhi by train for the five hour trip, travelling third class. It is very hot and dusty, and the train is much overcrowded. Hara Pugni-valla climbs to an upper bunk to make more room, and in his half-reclining position, he sort of suspends himself there, mildly grinning the whole time. He intrigues me, this middle-aged Sikh from the village, making a trip to the city only five hours away for the first time in his life. He speaks not a word of English so I cannot talk directly with him. But I want to find out how his head works, so with Bhai as my translator, I put to him the first of many questions.

"If you had three wishes, what would they be?"

He just looks at me, like it's a non-question. I fix my gaze, determined to get an answer. Finally he speaks. "The goddess is not going to grant me three wishes."

Hold on! Who said anything about a goddess!

...oh, yeah.

I put the question to him again. "If the goddess were to give you three things, what would you ask her for?"

Well! The goddess isn't about to give him anything! He isn't deserving of anything because he isn't leading a good life. Et cetera, et cetera, et cetera....

"Okay, let's suppose you have lived a most exemplary life and as a reward, the goddess will grant you *one* thing. What will you ask for?"

Long pause.

Deep reflection.

Then a determined response as though the saying of it would make it so. "I would ask her for a new wife. My wife is a bitch!"

Interesting....

We are met at the train station by Bhai's brother who takes us to the village on his tractor. After a meal of goat curry, chapatis and home made brew—and a good night's sleep on string-woven beds under the open sky—we travel by ox-cart to a farther village for the wedding ceremony.

It is one of those traditional arranged marriages where the bride and groom have never met. Immediately upon our arrival, the father of the bride—with great pride—takes me aside to show me a room stacked to the ceiling with furniture and crockery and linen: it is costing this man a bundle for a dowry to get the first of three daughters married off.

I return to the courtyard where the festivities are in progress. People are in a fun-loving mood. The women express appreciation that I am wearing traditional Punjabi dress, but are not impressed with the size of my earrings. They take it upon themselves to replace the tiny studs with huge gold rings, the diameters of which are much too large for the small openings of my pierced ears.

While all this is going on, the young bride remains secluded. After my earring ordeal, I enter the small room where she sits alone. She is a beautiful girl and looks stunning in the traditional red wedding sari—but she is so young! Does she have any dreams, I wonder, any thoughts about the possibilities for her life? She gives no clues. She remains silent, even motionless, displaying neither anticipation nor resistance.

It is one of those traditional arranged marriages where the bride and groom have never met.

At the appropriate moment two female relatives come to fetch the bride. They drape a blanket over her and lead her out to the waiting groom. While she remains hidden from view, they pull her hand from beneath the blanket and tie it with a string to the hand of her new husband. I whisper to Bhai, "What if she doesn't like him?"

"Oh, she'll like him," he replies, nonchalantly.

"Yes, but what if she doesn't?"

"No," he giggles, "she will."

"But, I mean, just suppose now that against all odds, for some totally unforeseen and unanticipated reason, she just doesn't take to him?"

Without hesitation comes the reply. "Well, she wouldn't let on because she wouldn't want to disappoint her family." Then my host sings a song to the new bride. "Go away now, to your new village and to your new family," the lyrics instruct. "Do your duties there very well, so you will not bring shame to your family."

The ceremonies and feasting over, the groom's relatives file back inside their rented bus, on top of which is now stacked the furniture and crockery and linen. The new bride, still draped under her blanket and tied by a string to her new husband, is led to the back seat of a car. "When will she get to see him?" I ask Bhai.

"Oh," he replies casually, "he'll lift up the blanket and take a peek on the way home." It's an interesting response, but not an answer to my question. I guess he just can't see it from the girl's point of view.

It's fascinating. First, there's Hara Pugni-valla. I think of his wife, tied for life to a man who feels little or no regard for her. Now this young girl, tied (literally) to a man she does not even know! What possible life can these women have? They are traded away—and not even in an exchange they can feel good about. Their fathers have had to fork over a room full of furniture and crockery and linen to get someone to take them away. Chattels!

What possible life can these women have? They are traded away—and not even in an exchange they can feel good about.

And what awaits the young bride in her new household? What is she being taken there to do? She will labour long and hard under the tutelage of a mother-in-law who may be very critical of the way she has been taught to do things. She will be regarded as the lowest-ranking member of her husband's family, at least until she can bear him a son, or until an even younger girl is married into the household. Moreover, she may well be the unwitting victim of domestic abuse and, if one of the really unlucky ones, add to the rising statistics of death by bride-burning. Guess who's gonna be dinner!

Such promise of future excellence turned into indiscriminate mingling. *Promise* to *promiscuity.* Thank goodness *we* don't have arranged marriages with dowry or brideprice. Thank goodness *we* don't treat women like they're some kind of possession. Thank goodness *we* don't treat them like a commodity and bury their identity beneath a pile of furniture and crockery and linen.

Oh yeah? What is going on, culturally speaking, when a woman is "joined" to a man? An exchange from one male (father) to another (husband), that's what! "Who gives this woman to be with this man?" recites the cleric. The father dutifully answers, "I do." And what happens the very instant the vows are repeated? The groom is invited to take possession of his new property: "You may now kiss the bride," allows the cleric, and the groom lifts the "blanket" to "take a peek".

After the young woman has put her signature to the deal, what does the cleric proudly declare? Nothing less than the loss of her name and identity! "And now I present to you Mr. and Mrs. John Jones."

Mrs?. . . John?. . . Jones?.... *Who* is that?! Everyone smiles and claps their hands and shouts "Congratulations!". Chattels!

Mrs?. . . John?. . . Jones?.... Who is that?!

And what will meet the young Western bride in her new environment? Well, for a start, she will probably carry on two jobs at the same time, one in the marketplace where she will likely work long and hard under the tutelage of her male counterparts and receive less than equal pay, and another in the home, where she will perform domestic duties largely on her own, with no benefits and little recognition. If she devotes her full energy to the role of wife and mother, she will soon feel the stigma of being "just a housewife", where the recognition is lesser still. Moreover, she may well be the unwitting victim of domestic abuse and, if one of the really unlucky ones, add to the rising statistics of death by wife-beating. Guess who's gonna be dinner!

"Marriage," said Mae West, "is a fine institution—but I'm not ready for an institution yet!"

Not in *any* culture.

"I have laboured to make the murderers of females ashamed of themselves; and have heard their cowardly cruelty defended by the assertion that such victims were doubly good—because they ate well, and because of the distress it caused their husbands and friends."

—Rev. Thomas Williams

WHAT'S EATING THE COOK

From STORY
(a tale)

To HISTORY
(lived events)

What's eating the cook? Captain Cook, that is. I'm at Kealakekua Bay on the big island of Hawaii. There's a monument here to the famous Captain, marking the spot where he was killed by the Hawaiians.

Cook first sailed this way in 1776, visiting Kauai and Niihau. A year later, after a voyage to Vancouver, he came back with his two ships, *Resolution* and *Discovery,* and made a clockwise circumnavigation around this big island. The Hawaiians were particularly pleased to see him; they waved as he sailed along their coastline and beckoned him to come ashore. When Cook and his men landed here at Kealakekua Bay, they were met and escorted to the settlement with great excitement. Cook was especially well-attended; the Hawaiians treated him with great respect, feasting him and serving him the ceremonial drink of kava.

Why did the Hawaiians kill Captain Cook?

The feasting went on for a number of days. Then the Hawaiians began asking their honoured guest when he would be leaving. When Cook replied his departure was imminent, the Hawaiians seemed much relieved. Cook did leave, saying he would return the following year. As fate would have it, however, soon under sail in these blue Pacific waters, the *Resolution* sprung her foremast, so Cook directed his ships to return to Kealakekua Bay so the vessel could be repaired.

This time the Hawaiians did not seem at all glad to see them. In fact, the natives were very anxious about the whole affair. They remained quiet—but they did pillage a bit. Then someone stole the cutter from the *Discovery*, and at this inconvenience, Cook got angry and went ashore to "find the chief". The Hawaiians tried to stop him, and when he resisted, they killed him.

Why did the Hawaiians kill Captain Cook? It had to do with confusing *story* with *history*: the *story* of the lost god-chief *Lono* with the *history* of the annual festival of the Makahiki. In Hawaiian mythology, *Lono* is associated with the founding chiefs of the islands who were born of sacred mothers and married to sacred wives. Theirs was the original power over the fertility of the land. In real or imagined time, these chiefdoms were lost to upstart rulers who were worshippers of the god *Ku*. The paramount chief of Hawaii at the time of Cook's explorations here was Kalaniopuu of the line of *Ku*. The lost god-chief *Lono*, however, was believed indespensible to the rulers of *Ku* because of *Lono's* ongoing mythological control over fertility of the land. And it was at the annual festival of the Makahiki that *Lono* would return to Hawaii to renew the fertility of the land, claim it as his own, only to be superceded again by the ruling chief of *Ku*.

The extraordinary thing about this incident is that the Hawaiians could have gone so far without distinguishing between myth and reality.

The treatment the Hawaiians accorded Captain Cook corresponded to this story about their god. Cook's visit to Hawaii coincided with the annual return of *Lono* and with the manner in which the legendary god-chief would return—in a "right circuit" around the big island of Hawaii and a landing here at Kealakekua Bay, the site of Hikiau, the main temple of *Lono*. When Cook arrived, the Hawaiians prostrated themselves before him, chanting "Lono", and they presented food and kava both to him and to the image of the god.

The Makahiki festival lasts for 23 days, after which time the image of *Lono* suffers a ritual death. It was toward the end of the 23 day period that the Hawaiians began to ask Cook when he would be leaving. His imminent departure was, once again, right on ritual schedule according to the story. *Lono* would leave and the reigning *Ku* chief would reassume power. But when Cook returned unexpectedly and came ashore "to find the chief", the story was altered: *Lono* had returned to depose the existing ruler and to reinstate the former line of chiefs in Hawaii. Viewed within the context of the story, this represented an aggressive military act—and Cook could not be allowed to succeed.

Didn't it occur to them somewhere along the line that this pasty-skinned European was not their god?

The extraordinary thing about this incident is that the Hawaiians could have gone so far without distinguishing between myth and reality—between *story* and *history*. Didn't it occur to them somewhere along the line that this pasty-skinned European was not their god? How could anyone be so thoroughly blinded by a belief system? It's preposterous! These ancient Hawaiians must have been a breed unto themselves!

Hold on. What about the Crusades and the Holy Wars? Didn't we also let our belief systems push us over the brink? And not just in ancient history, either. What about the extermination of six million Jews in Hitler's Germany, the killing fields in Kampuchea, the squashing of the pro-democracy movement in China, the genocide (still going on) in East Timor.... Then there's South Africa, Northern Ireland, Bosnia, Georgia, Czechnya, Rwanda, Zaire.... And remember the nuclear arms race? Risking the very future of a living planet over a few out-moded ideas!

Yes, a whole lot of awful things have been done—and are still being done—in the name of religion and ideology. We kill and die for our belief systems. We bring unbearable suffering to ourselves and our neighbours because we fail to distinguish between myth and reality....

Just as with Captain Cook, a myth may well be the death of us.

In 1850, Tuikilakila inflicted a severe blow on his old enemies the Natewans, when nearly one hundred of them were slain, among whom was found the body of Ratu Takesa, the King's own cousin. The Chiefs of the victorious side endeavoured to obtain permission to bury him, since he held the high rank of Rakesa, and because there was such an abundance of bokola. "Bring him here," said Tuikilakila, "that I may see him." He looked on the corpse with unfeigned delight. 'This,' said he, 'is a most fitting offering to Na Tavasara (the war-god). Present it to him: let it then be cooked, and reserved for my own consumption. None shall share with me. Had I fallen into his hands, he would have eaten me: now that he has fallen into my hands, I will eat him.' And it is said that he fulfilled his word in a few days, the body being lightly baked at first, and then preserved for repeated cooking."

—Rev. Thomas Williams

Recipe # 26

THEY'LL JUST DIE LAUGHING

From **MUSE**
(to contemplate)

To **AMUSEMENT**
(a form of
distraction)

Canada Place. A hotel and convention centre on Vancouver's spectacular harbourfront. It's a gorgeous autumn evening; the lights of the north shore of the harbour stand out against the coastal mountains and glisten in the sea. Just off the reception area in the spacious lobby is a classy bar with smoked-glass windows reaching to the sky. Music floats from a shiny black grand piano: "Somewhere over the rainbow, way up high...."

I'm in a meeting room down the hall, invited here as one of about fifty people to consider a critical path. Our host has not called us together wistfully. One can tell he has given it a great deal of thought, for he is not ordinary in any sense of the word. He is a speaker, a writer, a publisher, a businessman—and very good at all of them. At sixty, with thick white hair, he tells us he has just seen his first grandchild, and he does not want the infant to grow up a tenant in his own land.

That is the course his country, Canada, is taking. Its duly elected government is signing away much of its political and economic sovereignty in bilateral and multilateral trade agreements that favour big business and American-based multinational corporations. As strange as it sounds, Canada is willingly surrendering its independence, giving up its ability to set and maintain a national agenda. In short, it is dissolving itself into the United States of America.

"Give me a better idea," he begs of us, "because the last thing I want to do is start another political party—but I see no other way...." I have no better idea—nor has anyone else in the room. By the end of the evening we take a straw vote: all but a few urge him onto the political trail. The dissenters can be forgiven; they are primarily members of his own family.

I keep thinking about it though, because the implications are staggering. Another political party will split the vote even more—and we all know what happens to idealistic people once they move into the political arena. Democracy in practice, as Noam Chomsky points out, is a game of the elite.*

As strange as it sounds, Canada is willingly surrendering its independence.

A few weeks later I meet him again. He is giving another one of his superb talks with barely a note in hand. Then he listens patiently and responds to the myriad of questions from the floor, and graciously converses with the handful of hangers-on as he tries to exit. He is tired and his voice is giving out. We drive him back to his hotel.

"I have an idea," I say to him. "Why don't you do the 'Larry King Live' thing on Canadian television? It could be a true fifth estate and you could take on the lot of them. You could take Chretien to task for his weak stand on the Free Trade Agreement. You could challenge the New Democratic Party to act. You could put tough questions to Government. You could be independent of any political party and beholden to no one. You could be the conscience of...."

"You could never do that kind of programming on Canadian television," comes his reasoned reply. "The media in this country is controlled by such a small elite. They would never allow you to do it."

On reflection, I realize he is right. Not only are the media controlled by the elite, the media *are* the elite. Television stations—apart from the publicly-funded CBC and provincial educational channels—are owned by corporations. Many of those corporations are in turn owned by or affiliated with larger corporations—all one big happy family. The government of the day—backed by the same family compact—has cut funding to the CBC to the point that it, too, is dependent on commercial revenue for its discretionary spending—and guess who buys most network commercials!

Canadian television is following in the footsteps of its counterpart south of the border. Obsessed with audiences and markets, it programs for distraction. We fill our airwaves with a glut of America's formula sit-coms, banal dramas and cheap game shows. The ones we do not import outright, we imitate. The attempt at information programming fares only marginally better. Canada's fifth estate—electronic journalism—is too often pseudo-information about pseudo-events and pseudo-people.

Television is packaged in a way that appeals, so much so that viewers actually believe they are being informed and entertained. "They get what they want", not realizing they have been conditioned to want what they get. It's the perfect recipe for marginalizing a population and reducing its capacity to respond, a fatal blend of Orwell's *1984* and Huxley's *Brave New World:*

Orwell, concerned people would be overcome by an externally-imposed oppressor;
Huxley, concerned people would come to love their oppression.

Orwell, concerned books would be banned;
Huxley, concerned there would be no need to ban books because no one would want to read them.

Orwell, concerned people would deprive us of information.
Huxley, concerned we'd be so over-loaded with information that we'd be reduced to passivity.

Orwell, concerned the truth would be concealed from us;
Huxley, concerned truth would be drowned in a sea of irrelevance.

Orwell, concerned we would become a captive people;
Huxley, concerned we would become a trivial people.

Orwell, concerned we could be controlled by inflicted pain;
Huxley, concerned we would be controlled by inflicted pleasure.

In short, Orwell was concerned that what we *hate* would ruin us; Huxley, concerned that what we *desire* would ruin us.

It's all summed up in a book Neil Postman wrote about television which he aptly titled, *Amusing Ourselves to Death.*** There are two ways a people can be destroyed, says Postman: one, by becoming imprisoned; the other, by becoming burlesqued.

Postman thinks television is most suited to mindless distraction. He suggests we make it one big laugh-in; then we would see how ridiculous it really is. Maybe so, but meanwhile, top government positions continue to be staffed by top business people, and the media continue to be owned by corporations which are in turn owned by larger corporations. The private control of public resources continues to go unchallenged. Transnational space—mass communication, data processing, information transmission—is concentrating in private hands, largely outside the control of *any* government. Dominant elites have developed a new legal framework to exploit and control.

Anyone challenging the system is labelled and dismissed, and public outcry is quickly drowned out by the laughter of the electronic cabaret. Sit-coms...soap operas...game shows.... They'll just die laughing.

muse *v.* to think, to contemplate; *n.* a source of inspiration:
amusement *v.* idling away time; *n.* a form of distraction.

Instead of *musing* ourselves to life, we are *amusing* ourselves to death.

Anyone challenging the system is labelled and dismissed, and public outcry is quickly drowned out by the laughter of the electronic cabaret.

A new political party, valiantly and ideally designed to stem the tide, seems doomed to failure. Even in the context of one relatively small country like Canada, it is too little, too late. Or is it too big, too early? Hmmm....

'When the bodies of enemies are procured for the oven, the event is published by a peculiar beating of the drum, which alarmed me even before I was informed of its import. Soon after hearing it, I saw two canoes steering for the island, while someone on board struck the water, at intervals, with a long pole, to denote that they had killed someone. When suffi-ciently near, they began their fiendish war dance, which was answered by the indecent dance of the women. On the boxed end of one of the canoes was a human corpse, which was cut adrift and tumbled into the water soon after the canoe touched land, where it was tossed to and fro by the rising and falling waves until the men had reported their exploit, when it was dragged ashore by a vine tied to the left hand. A crowd, chiefly females, surrounded the dead man, who was above the ordinary size, and expressed most unfeelingly their surprise and delight. 'A man truly! A ship! A land!' The warriors, having rested, put a vine around the other wrist of the bokola...and two of them dragged it, face downwards, to the town, the rest going before and performing the war-dance....".

—Rev. Thomas Williams

Recipe # 27
MAKING HEADCHEESE

SENATUS
Universitatis
Omnibus has Literas perlecturis Salutem

From **UNIVERSE**
(the whole)

To **UNIVERSITY**
(an institution for "hire" learning)

My love affair with higher education begins when I am very young—not that my chances of getting any are good. In fact, I hardly ever go to school because I am part of a family professional logrolling act, and we are on the road most of the time. That turns out to be an advantage, actually, because you have to drop out of school now and then if you want to get an education.

Home, when I am there, is rural Nova Scotia and that's where the decisive event takes place. It's Sunday; I am 11 years old. A missionary on furlough comes to speak at our village church. He has just spent six years in India. He tells us about all the false gods they have over there and about their very primitive notions of medicine. For example, there is a local healer, he says, who grows the nail of the small finger on his right hand about three inches long so he can reach down and clean out the throats of people with respiratory infections. I never forget that. Then he says the benediction in Hindi and that really "blows my mind".

You have to drop out of school now and then if you want to get an education.

The missionary is encouraging people to go to India, and I think that's my style, so years later, when I graduate from high school, I take a Bachelor's degree in Psychology, minoring in Theology, at Mount Allison University in Canada's Maritime provinces. In the course of translating the Bible from Hebrew, I "read between the lines": I discover the old Testament is an anthropological monograph about a group of pastoral nomads in the Middle East. At the same time, I am immersing myself in Comparative Religion and am fast realizing there's a lot to be said for other great traditions like Hinduism and Buddhism.

Take the Hindu notion of *Brahman-Atman:* "Endless change without, and at the heart of the change an abiding reality—*Brahman.* Endless change within, and at the heart of the change an abiding reality—*Atman*". Were there then two realities? No, answered the yogis, *Brahman* and *Atman* are one and the same. It illuminates something Einstein said. "A human being is part of the whole, called by us the universe," he declared, "a part limited in time and space." We experience ouselves, our thoughts and feelings as being separate. Einstein called this a kind of optical delusion of our consciousness—a "prison", which causes us to feel affection only to the people nearest to us. Our task, he said, must be "to free ourselves from this prison by widening our circle of compassion to embrace all living creatures."*

I also like the non-aggressive, philosophical system expounded by the Buddha: "There is suffering. There is the origin of suffering. There is the cessation of suffering. There is the path to the cessation of suffering." Buddhism demands no blind faith, claims no dogmatic creeds, engages in no rites and ceremonies. It provides a clear path of discipline through pure thinking and pure living to gain wisdom and enlightenment. Throughout its 2500 year history, no drop of blood has been shed in the name of the Buddha. No monarch has wielded the sword on his behalf. No conversion has been achieved through forceful means.**

During all my years of theological education, the other students in the program do not seem to be unsettled by things they are learning. They've got a career plan and that's that. Nothing seems to be happening to them on any other level. It's like they aren't figuring it out! They go right on expounding Christianity as the one true religion. Why can't they see?

Of course, by now I know I can't be a missionary—but I'm still concerned about the guy who puts his finger down people's throats. So I choose a more practical path—and a change of scenery to boot. I take a Masters degree in Social Work at the University of British Columbia on Canada's west coast where I concentrate on international development.

I travel to Southeast Asia and the Pacific islands, studying foreign aid programs run by governments and international voluntary agencies. When I see what's happening, I know I can't do development either. The aid programs are destroying indigenous patterns of living and pulling local populations into the vortex of Western culture.

Like the theologians, the development people I meet do not seem to be unsettled by the things that are happening. They have a career plan and that's that. They go from one development project to another, seemingly unaware of the cultural dimensions of their actions. Why can't they see?

The aid programs are destroying indigenous patterns of living and pulling local populations into the vortex of Western culture.

They can't see...because they're *inside* it. That's it—the old "fish don't see water" thing. I've got to get outside the fish bowl! I've got to get a handle on *culture* because by now I see it has us doing some pretty funny stuff—like sticking our fingers down other people's throats, both literally and metaphorically.

So I take a Doctoral degree in Anthropology. I return to the South Pacific to find out everything I can about the early missionaries to Fiji and the foreign aid people who are in there today. That will give me insight into the two things I almost ended up doing: missionary work and cross-cultural development aid.

And guess what? I discover they're the same thing! One is just a secular version of the other. The missionaries came with their *charity* (money) and set up *missions* in order to *convert* the Fijians. The development people come with their *foreign aid* (money) and set up *agencies* in order to *individuate* the Fijians. *Charity* and *foreign aid* mean a shift from trading stuff with your kin to buying and selling stuff with anybody. *Missions* and *agencies* mean a shift from taking orders from chiefs to taking responsibility yourself. *Conversion* and *individuation* mean a shift from something like ascribed status to something like achieved status. These three areas of social life—economic, political and ideological—are critical aspects of our Western culture that we unwittingly if not willingly inflict on others.

Again, during all my years of anthropological education, my fellow students do not seem unsettled by things they are learning. They select this or that culture, specialize in myth or ritual or symbol, formulate a research question, write up a fieldwork proposal...but they don't connect what they are researching to the issue of culture, *per se*. Nothing seems to be happening to them at that level. They aren't figuring anything out! They are satisfied to use anthropological theories to justify the way society is rather than to liberate people from it. To me, Anthropology is beginning to look a lot like "anthro-apology". Why can't they see!

Culture...has us doing some pretty funny stuff. Like sticking our fingers down other people's throats, both literally and metaphorically.

Theology, Development, Anthropology: all my fields of study seem to coalesce into the same thing. Maybe my approach is at fault—or maybe it's the University....

Yes, maybe it's the way education is converted into training and intelligence is converted into compliance; or the way universities market higher education as a commodity, and fashion the curriculum as a catalogue for educational consumers. Maybe it's the way information and knowledge get artificially fragmented into increasingly smaller and more isolated bits and fields and specializations, until independent and holistic thinking are all but impossible. Yes, we have reduced *higher* education to *hire* education, turning universities into training institutions and factories for making "headcheese".

What a pity! I mean, where better to study the "universe" than in the "universe-city". But that's not what today's "universe-cities" are about. They're busy turning out graduates whose chief interest is to find security, become somebody important, or have "the good life" with as little thought as possible. The urge to be successful, the search for security, the desire for comfort: these things, says the modern sage, Krishnamurti, smother discontent, put an end to spontaneity and breed fear. Fear blocks intelligent understanding of life and dullness of mind sets in.***

I know now I cannot stay in the university—but there is still something about Theology and Anthropology that won't let me be. Whatever that something is, it gets lost when you compartmentalize it and run it through an institution of "hire" learning. I must study them again as though I were never taught at a university. I must get underneath the theories, the concepts, the opinions, the tenets and dogma and doctrines. I must get the total picture.

Information and knowledge get artificially fragmented into increasingly smaller and more isolated bits and fields and specializations, until independent and holistic thinking are all but impossible.

But where do I start? Let's see, what did we have before we had Theology? Well, we had a *story* about our relationship with God. And what did we have before we had Anthropology? We had a *history* about our relationship with each other. Interesting: the "preaching" of Jesus was encoded into *parables* (story) and the "teaching" of Marx was decoded from *dialectic* (history). Jesus used the *art* of *story*; Marx, the *science* of *history*. Is it possible that what anthropologists failed to see in the science of history is parallel to what theologians failed to see in the art of the story?

Now, before my Anthropology colleagues get all upset, I'm not suggesting that Marx was the founder of Anthropology.

He wasn't, any more than Jesus was the founder of Christianity. I would hasten to add, however, that Marx would have made a very fine Anthropologist—and Jesus a very fine Christian.

With my new suspicion about the parallel between Anthropology and Theology in mind, I return to Fiji and ask a different set of questions. What might these Methodist missionaries among the cannibals of Fiji have achieved, had they realized the lesson of the "story" (parable)? And what might the development people achieve here now if they realized the lesson of "history" (dialectic)? This time I get a very different answer: they could (have) help(ed) people to "shift the direction of their look". In the parables of Jesus, the process is threefold: you encounter a situation (Event), you change your perspective (Reversal), and you act according to the new insight (Decision). In the dialectic of Marx, the process is also threefold: you encounter a situation (Negation), you change your perspective (Reinterpretation), and you act according to the new insight (Affirmation). Once again, only the language has changed.

Encountering an event in Theology or a negation in Anthropology both involve an act of *suspicion*. Things are not as they appear; there is something about the situation that is not real. Similarly, making a reversal in Theology or a reinterpretation in Anthropology both involve an act of *illumination*. There is something to be seen through. Finally, making a decision in Theology or an affirmation in Anthropology involves an act of *liberation*. There is a state of freedom to be attained by getting outside the social system. Separately or taken together, Theology and Anthropology could offer an end to ideology—freedom from the constraints of the social world.

Yes, it's not Theology or Anthropology that are amiss! It's how we have subverted them—and every other discipline—to serve the productive needs of society. We turn every discipline, every path of inquiry into a commodity. In the process, we fail to see that Anthropology is an emancipatory social science and Theology is no less concerned with the same goal. Both of them are about seeing through "false gods" and preventing people from putting their fingers down other people's throats. I now understand why I was attracted to these two disciplines in the first place.

We turn every discipline, every path of inquiry into a commodity.

Well, I write an academic treatise about this for which I have been awarded a prestigious post-doctoral fellowship. At the culmination of the fellowship period, I am invited to a dinner at the University Faculty Club along with other recipients. It's a chance for us to meet the donors, and the professors who have served on the Selection Committee.

It's a grand occasion, complete with receiving line. After all, we are, as the University President tells us in his short address, *"la creme de la creme."* We represent disciplines ranging from biochemistry to ethnomusicology and we are researching some pretty heady stuff: "microwave spectroscopy of gaseous molecules", "electropharmacology of the neuronal mascarinic receptor", "investigations on lipid-protein interactions in relation to molecular mechanisms of anaesthesia", "studies on the control of microsomal enzymes in rat liver by hepatic steroid binding proteins"....

And me? I'm studying missionaries...

...in Fiji.

Theology and Anthropology could offer an end to ideology—freedom from the constraints of the social world.

I am introduced to the Selection Committee: chemists and physicists and geologists and a lone social scientist who says to me, "Why did it have to be about missionaries! Do you realize how hard it is to convince these physical scientists to give a post-doctoral fellowship to someone who wants to study missionaries!"

I can imagine, especially when the missionaries I'm studying are all dead! The only "concrete evidence" I come across are the bones of the first missionary to Fiji. The church erected on his gravesite was destroyed in a hurricane, so they dug up his bones and placed them in a box until they can rebuild the church and give him a proper Christian burial. (Descendants of cannibals are going to give the missionary a Christian burial!) In the meantime, the bones are just sitting there in a small administrative office on the island of Taveuni—but it's neither here nor there.

So I'm at this formal dinner. I'm introduced to the members of the donor family. What is my discipline, they promptly ask.

"Anthropology."

"So what kind of animal do you study?"

I laugh. Then I realize it's a serious question. "Human animals," I offer.

"Have you found any bones yet?"

I laugh. Then I realize it's a serious question. "Yes," I reply, "as a matter of fact, I have."

university n. sing. a place where they take *la creme de la creme* and turn it into headcheese.

You have to drop out of school now and then if you want to get an education.

"Rare cases are known in which a Chief has wished to have part of the skull of the enemy for a soup-dish or drinking-cup, when orders are accordingly given not to strike that man in the head."

—Rev. Thomas Williams

Recipe # 28

USING LEFTOVERS

From HIRE
(payment for service)
To HIERARCHY
(classified
according to rank)

One cannot traverse the great subcontinent of India without seeing them. Some are modest structures with simple domes, others massive compounds with ornately decorated towers. Most are unknown outside India, but a few are world famous—like the *Kalighat* temple in Calcutta where I witness the slaughter of a young goat as a blood sacrifice to the goddess Durga, or the great *Jagannath* temple at Puri where I gaze upon the massive wooden chariots used to escort the gods from one temple to another in their annual festival. Then there's the magnificent golden-domed *Minakshi* temple in Madurai where I watch the priests bathe the sacred golden images with milk before retiring them for the night. From north to south, whatever their size or decor, their purpose is singular: the Indian temples are the guardians of Hindu purity in the on-going quest for immortality. Without purity, there can be no relief from the endless cycle of reincarnation and rebirth. Purity is the key to immortality; in short, it buys time.

Purity is the "wealth" of institutionalized Hinduism. At the other end of the spectrum, the ultimate poverty is pollution. And there you have it: the essential dynamic of the Hindu caste system. It's a hierarchy of purity and pollution—Brahmins, Ksatriyas, Vaishas and Sudras, each caste less pure and more polluted than the one before. Within each caste there is a hierarchy of its own, with any number of sub-castes jostling for relative purity ranking. It is the game of push and pull in the marketplace of immortality.

None of this could be accomplished easily without someone to do the "dirty work". There you find them, outside the caste system altogether, existing in a more or less permanent state of pollution: the "Untouchables". They wash the clothes, repair the shoes, sweep the floors, clean the latrines, deal with soil, menstrual blood, faeces, urine.... In the process of purifying the world for the "insiders", they become pollution itself. As such, they are not allowed inside the Hindu temples. They are the leftovers in a society where time is *purity*. It is a correct but misplaced search for immortality....

The caste system is not like a class system. It's not a ladder. It's not even like a vertical hierarchy; it's more like...a *circular* one. It's a wheel! A wheel with timeless Brahma (God) at its spaceless, motionless centre; purest Brahminism at the hub; and a variety of caste and sub-caste groupings stretching out along its spokes where they encounter progressively more motion, more pollution, more existence in time and space. Then, outside "the wheel of life" altogether, we find the so-called Untouchables, who make up a protective outer rim, shielding those inside from the pollution of bodily existence. It's the outside of the wheel that gets pulled through the mud!

Cleanliness is next to godliness. And that just about sums up the Hindu caste system. But if in Indian society, time is purity, in Western society, time is *money*. Money is our counterpart to Hindu purity.

If in Indian society, time is purity, in Western society, time is money.

It all started when farming started. That's when we began piling up surplus goods and then using money as a symbol of that accumulated wealth. And that's when we abandoned the search for true and eternal Life in timeless Spirit by "farming" for it with time, using money as the symbol.

It sounds strange at first. You'd think our counterpart to an Indian temple would be a cathedral. Not so! Or at least not any more. Our temples are *banks*—yes, banks. It's not surprising when one discovers that the first banks were in fact temples and the first to issue money were priests or priest-kings, as in the great temple compounds of the Near East where large amounts of surplus grain and gold were given as offerings to the divine kings. This we know from inscriptions carved into the walls of the temples. In Greece, for example, temples held great amounts of property in the form of land, precious objects and coined money. The inscriptions also record leases and assignments, payments of rent and fines for default, loans and interest, and many other business transactions. Sounds like a bank to me!

So the early temples became the first banks, the early priests became banker-priests and later just plain bankers, and time became money: a correct but misplaced search for immortality.

You'd think our counterpart to an Indian temple would be a cathedral. Not so! Or at least not any more. Our temples are banks.

The money system is not like a class system. It's not a ladder. It's not even like a vertical hierarchy; it's more like...a *circular* one. It's a pie! A pie with absolute wealth at its centrepoint; a very few, very wealthy individuals and families making up "the inner circle"; with corporations and big business—owned or controlled by "insiders"—stretching out along its radii where managers of progressively decreasing rank do the bidding of the corporate elite. Outside the circle altogether, more or less permanently disenfranchised, are those who do "the dirty work", hirelings who labour to keep the money concentrated at the centre. As people are pushed toward the outer crust, they encounter progressively more struggle, more competition, more control over their freedom, their space, their time. For no matter how you slice it, the pie is always cut from the centre and those at the outer rim get only the crust and the crumbs.

Eventually, the big picture emerges—and it's not a pretty one. In "developed" countries like the United States, Britain, Canada and New Zealand, for example, the richest 5 per cent own half the national wealth! The poorest 50% get by on less than 5% of the resources! Leftovers—in a society where time is money.

Money, like purity, is a substitute for real power and real life. Once golden images could be minted into coins, cosmic power could fall into the hands of just about anyone—and it did. Now we can traffic in immortality without ever having to go to a temple.

But there is only so much room at the centre. And money—like purity—remains the scarce commodity in the market-place of immortality. The goat sacrifice in the *Kalighat* temple of Calcutta is like the way we bleed ourselves in the market-place. The great chariots of the *Jagannath* that transport the sacred images are like the armoured trucks that move money from one bank to another. The washing of the golden images with milk in the *Minakshi* temple is like laundering "profits" after "milking the system". A correct but misplaced search for immortality.

Instead of using purity (money) to make a vertical tran-scendence to higher mental states, we make the circular ac-cumulation of purity (money) an end in itself. More purity (more money) means more life—and absolute purity (abso-lute money) means absolute life. We have a tremendous ca-pacity for self-deception.

Someone once asked the great world teacher, Krishnamurti, this question: "Should the Untouchables be allowed in the temples?" Without hesitation he replied, "There should be no temples."

 *"A Chief would kill a man or men on laying down a keel for a canoe, and try to add one for each fresh plank. These were always eaten as 'food for the carpenters'."*

—Rev. Thomas Williams

Recipe # 29
ONE LAST BONE TO PICK

From **BODY**
(the physical
structure of a
human being)

To **SOMEBODY**
(a person of
importance)

Egypt: cradle of civilization, land of the pharoahs, home of the pyramids.... I take a taxi from my hotel in downtown Cairo to the site of the ancient monuments. En route, the driver tells me it's a long distance from the entrance gate to the pyramids themselves. Too far to walk, he says, so would I like to take a camel—he just happens to have a friend who has a camel.... I resist his offer. Reluctantly, he drops me at the entrance gate which is only steps from the pyramids: unfortunately for him, I have been here before.

Three great pyramids...monuments to antiquity, rising out of a vast and silent desert.

It was about a decade before. That's when I saw the mummified bodies of the great pharoahs at the Egyptian Museum in Cairo. They are no longer on display, but back then one could gaze into the glass "coffins" of these ancient rulers. There they rested, silent testimonies of human history, encased in layer upon layer of treated linen. But time and natural elements had caused the cloth to decay, revealing the skeletal structures and exposing what remained of their hands and feet. The immortal pharoahs of Egypt, reduced to a pattern of bones....

A decade later and I stand once again beside the tombs that were to have housed their bodies forever. The pyramid of Cheops was built almost five thousand years ago with two and a half million blocks of stone, each weighing at least a couple of tonnes. It has been estimated that it took ten years to build the causeway and the massive earth ramps to move the stones, then another 20 years to raise the pyramid itself. Corps of masons and stonecutters, surveyors and mathematicians supervised 100,000 labourers assembled to do the backbreaking work.

Beside it is the pyramid of his son, Kephren, appearing larger because it is on higher ground but actually built to a lesser scale out of respect for the father. Then there's the pyramid of Mycerinus, which still bears some of its limestone slab covering. These three great pyramids are flanked by hundreds of mastaba-tombs built for lesser members of the royal family, nobles and other high-ranking people—monuments to antiquity, rising out of a vast and silent desert....

There are more than a few tour buses. First-time visitors gasp at the sheer size of the pyramids, and they take scores of photographs. Some of the more hearty make their way into the deep bowels of Kephren. It's hot and dark in the low, narrow passageway; the frightened and claustrophobic have to turn back.

There is no one in the inner chamber when I get here, only silence. An empty sarcophagus sits in a hollow space that housed some of the funerary items to be used in the afterlife. Above and around me are 60 million tonnes of stone. The air is stagnant, a subtle reminder that one ought not to linger.

There is no one in the inner chamber when I get here, only silence.... Above and around me are 60 million tonnes of stone.

I can only imagine the treasures that lay here and in the other chambers of this tomb before grave-robbers got their hands on them. The loot would have been sizeable compared to that of the young Pharoah Tutankhamun, who ruled for only nine years and was buried in the Valley of the Kings. The funerary treasures found there—in an insignificant Pharoah's tomb—are astounding! They fill twelve rooms in the Egyptian Museum.

Among the Treasures of Tutankhamun were found: one hundred, forty-three amulets and pieces of jewelry discovered among the wrappings of the king's body; a pair of gold sandals which were on the feet of the mummy; two innermost coffins, one of gilded wood and the other of solid gold; the now-famous exquisite mask of beaten gold inlaid with lapis lazuli and other gems; the gilded wooden shrines which fitted inside each other and held the gold sarcophagus; Tutankhamun's bed, covered with sheet gold; beautifully carved model ships, to be used by the Pharoah on his voyage through the afterworld; his wooden clothing chest and his wooden throne, covered with sheet gold, silver, gems and glass; papyrus paintings; chests of ebony and redwood, ceremonial wooden chairs, decorative stools, all inlaid with ivory and gold; miniature gold coffins inlaid with coloured glass and carnelian; carved wooden figures of the Pharoah; necklaces and bracelets and rings of solid gold encrusted with lapis lazuli, inlaid glass and other precious stones.... Altogether, about one thousand, seven hundred items were unearthed. Did they really think you can take it with you?

We spend a lifetime preparing for a "deathtime", doing things that will make us "timeless".

Then there is the mummification process itself. It took seventy days and involved a number of stages. First they extracted the brain by breaking it up and removing it through the nasal passage. Next they made an incision in the abdomen and removed the viscera (except for the heart and kidneys). They dehydrated the stomach, intestines, liver and lungs, and stored them separately in canopic jars. Then they sterilized the body and temporarily packed the internal cavities with natron and fragrant resins, and left it for thirty-five days. After the temporary packing was removed, the body cavities were permanently packed with linen soaked in resin, bags of cinnamon and myrrh, and sawdust. Then they anointed the body with fragrant oils, covered the abdominal incision and treated the outer skin with molten resin. Finally, they wrapped it up, placing jewelry and protective amulets among the bandages.

Why did they go to such bother? Why did they surround dead bodies with enormous treasures? And why did they entomb them in massive pyramids? What is it about Egypt that could possibly account for this activity?

Well, what is Egypt? A vast desert with a river running through it—a river that floods annually. So very early on, the Egyptians had farming! Where you have farming, you have surplus! And where you have surplus, you have a correct but misplaced search for immortality!

That doesn't mean other folk cultures in the region— hunters/gatherers or nomadic tribespeople—did *not* have any concerns about dying. I'm sure they did. It just means we can't know a lot about what they were thinking because their lifestyles and technologies didn't allow them to reproduce their ideas in material form. In the case of Egypt, we can literally *see* what they were thinking—and what they were thinking was embedded in a mythology that promised to extend the brief span of a human lifetime into eternity. And the Egyptians literally moved mountains in their attempt to do it.

But in spite of the pyramids and the treasures and the mummies, in the end, the body was not alive. The ancient Egyptians must have been mad!

Yes, they were absolutely mad. But the madness is not peculiar to ancient Egypt. It's in all of us. It's just that in the case of Egypt, it showed up in a more conscious and blatant form. In our case, it's more repressed and subtle—and that's what makes our's so difficult to see.

We don't build pyramids. In place of a massive *stone tomb*, we place a modest *tombstone*—but in planting that single slab, we are also "farming" in immortality. We don't stuff valuables in the open space around our coffins (there are no luggage racks on a hearse)—but we nevertheless store up treasures; "He who has the most toys when he dies wins." And we don't pull our brains out through our noses. We go one better than the ancient Egyptians: we bust our brains trying to immortalize ourselves while we're still alive!

You don't believe me? Ask just about anybody what they want to be remembered for and the remarkable thing is that they will tell you! Instead of rejoicing to be "membered" as a living *body*—a physical human being within the great chain of life—we struggle to be "*re*-membered" as a dead *somebody*— a person of importance, distinct from the ongoing flow of egoless existence.

Ask just about anybody what they want to be remembered for, and the remarkable thing is that they will tell you!

As a result, we spend a lifetime preparing for a "deathtime", doing things that will make us "timeless"—things like authoring a book; winning a medal; getting a bridge, a building, or even a town named after us; achieving some kind of political stature so that our name will be enshrined in the history books; even having a child so we can carry on the family name....

(Did I say "authoring a book"? Oh, dear!)

We will do anything, in short, that will "stop the clock", that will allow us to live on after we are gone—in other words, anything that will keep death from "grinning in at the banquet". It's fascinating! We spend our lifetime trying to buy life time—turning a *body* into a *somebody*—as though immortality were "in our bones".

"The shinbones of all bokolas are valued, as sail needles are made of them. If these bones are short, and not claimed by a Chief, there is a scramble for them among the inferiors, who sometimes almost quarrel over them."
—Rev. Thomas Williams

COOKING ON THE GO

From **FUSION**
(merging different
elements into a union)

To **CONFUSION**
(mistaking one thing
for another)

Bali is perhaps the most famous island in the Indonesian archipelago. I'm in my early twenties and up to this point in my life, it's the most exotic place I've ever been: terraced rice fields, split-gate temples, sacred volcanoes, trance dances, shadow plays, rituals of exorcism....

I'm a guest of the Secretary of the Board of Culture. It's a rare opportunity because Bali *is* culture and I get an "inside" view. I'm invited to watch *gamelan* orchestras audition on the lawn outside the Secretary's home. I'm taken to the dance academy where young girls are meticulously instructed in the intricate movements of the *oleg* and the *legong*. I'm driven to remote villages to see their woodcarving, painting and handcrafted jewelry. I gaze at streams of sarong-draped women bearing elaborately decorated offerings to the temples. I listen as stories from the *Ramayana* and the *Mahabharata* come to life in colourful mask dramas. I stride to the altars of *Brahma* and *Vishnu* and *Shiva* through the split gates of *Basakih*, mother temple of Bali, high on the slopes of volcanic Mount Agung.

It is enchanting. It is artistry, symmetry, harmony, balance. It is "paradise". It is...unsettling! I don't know why, but there is something about it that is just too...I'm going to need time to figure this one out.

It is enchanting. It is artistry, symmetry, harmony, balance. It is "paradise". It is... unsettling!

Then an unforeseen event occurs. A relative of my host gets killed. His family members immediately consult a Brahmin priest who informs them that the second auspicious date for his cremation is far too distant; we must perform the ritual the day after tomorrow.

Preparations are hastily made: the offerings, the sarcophagus, the cremation tower.... The tower is intriguing. There is a lower part, a base, which rests on carrying poles; it represents the underworld. The upper edge of the base displays a mountain motif indicating the upper boundaries of the earth. On top are multiple roofs, representing receding heavens. In between the "nether world" and the "upper world" is an open space, the sphere for the dead man. It's a vertical tri-partition.

The design echoes that of a Balinese temple. It has a stone base, representing a tortoise entwined by two snakes, creatures of the nether world; multiple roofs, made from the fibre of the sugar palm, representing heaven—which is conceived as having a number of layers or levels; and a middle section, the contact place for the gods when they visit this world.

Come to think of it, their whole culture is set up on this tri-partition. Life is sandwiched between an upper world and a nether world, between something they call *kaja* ("east", but also "upwards, in the direction of the mountains"), referring to things that are divine and propitious, and *kelod* ("west", but also "downward, in the direction of the sea"), associated with things that are evil and negative. The lives of the Balinese are suspended between the two.

You can see this tri-partition on a horizontal plane as well, as in the layout of their dwelling compounds. They place the household temple *kaja* (east), the refuse heap *kelod* (west) and the living quarters in the middle. Similarly, in the village temple system, the temple of the dead is located *kelod* of the village. Once souls are purified through cremation, they are honoured in another temple *kaja* of the village. The assembly hall temple is located right in the centre. Intriguing....

On cremation day, guests assemble at the dead man's home. When we arrive, I see the body resting on a raised platform surrounded by offerings. They are such beautiful offerings—so uniform, so symmetrical...!

We share a noonday feast. Then a Brahmin priest, assisted by female relatives of the dead man, makes more offerings at the spot where the body will be removed from the house. All of a sudden, there is loud shouting and a number of male relatives rush toward the body, lift it from the platform and transport it to the sarcophagus inside the cremation tower.

The tower is resting on that huge bier constructed of bamboo poles. A priest and two female relatives step onto the bier, flanking the sarcophagus and its contents. Then about one hundred men hoist the entire apparatus onto their shoulders. I join others in the long procession line behind a white shroud carried by the women. A priest sprinkles rice offerings on the path ahead of us, and we set out on our march to the cremation ground.

It's all starting to make sense to me now. Balinese culture is a balancing act—between the forces of the upper world and the nether world. It's in their organization of space. It's in their rituals. It's in their literature, too, as in the dramatic struggle between the mystical creature, *Barong*, and the widow-witch, *Rangda*. Representing good and evil, right and wrong, health and sickness, life and death, *Barong* and *Rangda* constantly battle it out. In the end, neither wins; it always ends in a draw. Fascinating....

It's as though there were a giant grid suspended over the island...reaching from the underworld to the heavens.

Midway along the route, the procession stops short. I watch in awe as that cumbersome bier with its human cargo is rotated full circle! It's no mean undertaking to coordinate a hundred or so men beneath such a massive wooden structure; they must have a *very* good reason for doing it! I ask my host. "They are disorienting the spirit of the dead man," he replies, "so it will not be able to find its way back to the village."

Disorienting! That's it! Now it all falls into place—or should I say out of place. The unsettling thing about Balinese culture is that everything is oriented! Everything is in its place! Nothing must ever be out of place, nothing left to its own devices—nothing, including people!

I find out they have a word for this proper orientation. It's *kaiket*, and it means "to be tied". The Balinese are tied from birth to death to a complex network of duties, obligations, temples, people and things. It's as though there were a giant grid suspended over the island, a kind of three-dimensional map, stretching not only horizontally but also reaching from the underworld to the heavens.

Life "with strings attached". One giant puppet show with the world as the stage. If things get "out of order", if people get "out of place", life becomes a chaotic void. There's a word for that too; it is *paling*. To be *paling* is to be frightfully "untied". That's what they're doing to this dead man—they're "untying" him! They've had him "tied" all his life and now that he's dead, they want him "untied" so they can get him "tied" on another plane.

The Balinese have invented an elaborate cultural order as though there were no "natural order", as though nature were confusion.

The architecture; the rituals; the dances and the dramas; the uniform, symmetrical offerings: all are attempts to placate forces that can neither be allied nor vanquished. The Balinese have invented an elaborate cultural order as though there were no "natural order", as though nature were confusion.

They've got it backwards and upside down! Nature has infinite order, a fusion that merges all the different elements into union. It's their culture that creates disorder and confusion, by setting up oppositions—good/evil, beauty/ugliness, health/illness, life/death—and then associating the earthly plane with the negative forces. Evil, ugliness, illness, death: how can they think of the Earth this way!

We arrive at the cremation site. They place the bier with its tower upon the funeral pyre. They cut the shroud. They make some final prayers and offerings. They pour holy water on the corpse, letting the pots break upon the ground. Then a male relative sets the sarcophagus ablaze.

Why don't they see Earth as the *highest* order, as the source of good and beauty and health and life, instead of a battle theatre where Nature has to be ordered!

Of course, by now you're anticipating my western echo of this eastern conundrum—so here it is: we do one better than the Balinese. We superimpose an even more disastrous cultural order onto the natural one, creating endless confusion. We alter the course of great rivers, destroying natural habitats and sanctioning the extinction of living species. We cut down our last remaining old-growth forests, savaging ecosystems which took eons to perfect. We scar and gouge the landscape with clear-cut logging and open-pit mining, as though we were consciously committed to a scorched earth policy. Cooking on the go!

With our rituals of rape and pillage, we treat the Earth as a battleground, and Nature as something to be conquered. We then flatter our prowess with inventions like "wilderness management", "free enterprise", and "patented life-forms", all of them oxymorons, ranking right up there with "military intelligence", "holy wars", and "salvation army".

Yes, we've got ourselves oriented alright—but whereas the Balinese are suspended from a grid, we are tied to the bottom line. Our *kaiket* is sadly grounded in a mentality that proclaims "bigger is better" and "the only value in a tree is after it is cut down".

Whereas the Balinese are suspended from a grid, we are tied to the bottom line.

It shows up in our organization of space, too. Cities are

"developed" into patterns that curiously come to resemble the structure of cancer cells. Factories are at one end, refuse heaps at the other, and temples—banks—dominate the centre. Combatants and "troopers" are strategically encamped in suburban clusters: symmetrical houses on symmetrical streets. "Boxes, little boxes, they're all made of ticky-tacky, and they all look just the same...."

It shows up in our literature, too. Consider this poem by Tennyson:

Flower in the crannied wall,
  I pluck you out of the crannies,
I hold you here, root and all, in my hand,
  Little Flower—but if I could understand
What you are, root and all, and all in all,
  I should know what God and man is.

He kills the flower in order to understand it—as though the Earth were an object to be reduced, dissected, analyzed, ordered and consumed! Contrast that with this Zen poem by Chin-doba:

The mountain slopes crawl with lumberjacks,
  Axing everything in sight—
Yet crimson flowers
  Burn along the stream.

The flames engulf the cremation tower. We stand back from the heat and watch it burn. Some venture close and pose in front of the inferno to have their pictures taken.

How can we think of the Earth this way? Whatever happened to the mystic vision of the poet, William Blake:

To see the world in a grain of sand,
  And a heaven in a wild flower;
Hold infinity in the palm of your hand,
  And eternity in an hour.

"To see the world in a grain of sand"—which it is, and which we are! We are grains of sand grown to consciousness. "And a heaven in a wild flower." A flower represents a very long journey on the evolutionary path, and if we could today find out there in that vast cosmos a single planet that had reached this stage of evolution, we would be screaming to get there! We would shout that we have found paradise!

I hear a loud cracking sound. My host leans over to me and whispers that the skull has just exploded and now the spirit is free to ascend to the heavens.

"Hold infinity in the palm of your hand"— to transcend the boundaries, to get beyond all the artificial distinctions that we make. "And eternity in an hour"—which is to realize there is no yesterday and no tomorrow. There is only now— and now is eternity.

A priest keeps careful watch on the burning. His eyes follow the column of smoke trailing into the sky. After a time, the flames die down and people start to make their way back to the village.

It seems a tragedy the Balinese have to die in order to get themselves turned around. By comparison, our own failure at reorientation is more like a farce. For the Balinese, battles are histrionics that always end in a draw, while we march on, thinking we are winning the battles when in fact we are losing the war.

"In the foregoing details, all colouring has been avoided, and many facts, which might have been advanced, have been withheld. All the truth may not be told. But surely enough has been said.... The picture, without exaggerating, might have been far darker; but it is dark enough to awaken sympathy for a people so deplorably fallen, and to quicken an earnest longing that their full deliverance may be at hand."

—Rev. Thomas Williams

PART III

TIME TO
TAKE STOCK

TOO MANY COOKS SPOIL THE BROTH

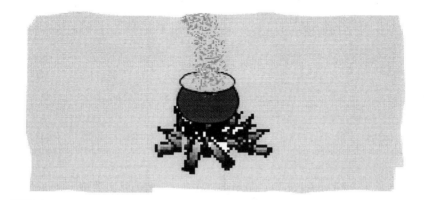

Time to take stock, to see through this thing called culture. But it is a difficult task because culture is the very thing we see through. How can we possibly see through what we see through—especially when what we see through isn't really there! How *do* you shatter an illusion, debunk a "false" consciousness, break a "spell"? In short, how do you get your hands on the secret ingredient in cannibal cookery?

How can we possibly see through what we see through—especially when what we see through isn't really there!

There's only one good reason to keep a secret: it gives considerable power and advantage to those who know it over those who do not, an advantage that would be lost "if the truth were known". The best-kept secrets are the ones that pay off handsomely: only a fool would reveal the location of a hidden treasure.

The secret ingredient in cannibal cookery is that kind of treasure, but only so long as it is hidden! It is time to "unearth the treasure" so that the "truth" may be known. And the truth starts where culture starts—at the very beginning: *as a society evolves, it gets caught in its need to survive in the particular form in which it has developed, and it almost always does this by ignoring the broader human needs that are common to people everywhere.* *

When I was teaching Anthropology I used a simulation game to illustrate this idea. I would divide a class of undergraduates into four groups, each receiving an envelope containing a few materials, a few tasks, and a few rules.

The materials consisted of coloured sheets of paper, pencils, rulers, paper clips and a pair of scissors. These "resources", however, were not equally distributed. One group would receive only a few sheets of paper and a ruler, for example, and there was a single pair of scissors. However, taken together, everything they needed to complete the tasks was supplied.

The tasks were very simple: cut a square of blue paper a certain size, cut a triangle of white paper another size, cut three rectangles of yellow paper and fasten them together with a paper clip.... The rules were equally straightforward: paper must be cut, not torn; all measurements must be accurate; only materials supplied can be used; exchanges between groups can be negotiated; the group first to complete all tasks is the winner.

These tasks could easily be executed by a five-year-old in as many minutes—but in all the times I used this game with university students, in no case did a group ever succeed within the allotted time. There was never a "winner". Had they simply shared the materials or joined to form one group, they could *all* have been winners—but never was it so hard to get one's hands on a pair of scissors!

As the game progressed, we would discover the emergence of "cultures" that curiously came to resemble a microcosm of the planet: First World, Second World, Third World—and within each "world", a Fourth World of difference. In a few short minutes, mature university students transformed themselves into competitive and rather unseemly little creatures. Power struggles and ideological conflicts broke out within groups as well as between them. And more than once were they on the verge of rebellion and revolution! There in a lecture room, these "normal" human beings acted out the same melodrama that daily fills the news reels: a human species on a planet with resources enough for everyone—but failing badly in their endeavours because of a distribution problem.

No group in any of those Anthropology classes ever said, "Let's play the game so we can't win"—but "can't win" they did! Similarly we don't say, "Let's set up the world so there will be lots of war and hardship and misery and starvation"—but that's what we get because of the way we distribute things! Nature provides the resources we need; it gives us some simple tasks to do, and time in which to do them; and there are a few hard rules. That's fair enough, but we have turned the joy of living into a struggle for survival by dividing ourselves into groups and distributing the resources unequally. The rest is history!

City states, empires, feudal states, monarchies, autocracies, colonization, genocide, ethnic cleansing, corporate control of the marketplace, third world exploitation.... Auschwitz, Kampuchea, Northern Ireland, Eritrea, East Timor, Rwanda, Chechnya, Sarajevo.... The mind-set of scarcity played out on the battlefield of life.

We have turned the joy of living into a struggle for survival by dividing ourselves into groups, and distributing the resources unequally.

Unequal distribution of resources creates a concentration of power which in turn sets into motion cultural institutions that reinforce and protect the inequalities. That, in a nutshell, is the truth of culture: the socially powerful exploiting the distribution system. These are the "cooks" who "spoil the broth"—and there are too many of them.

A WATCHED POT NEVER BOILS

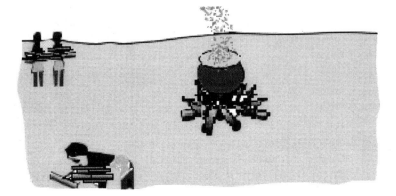

The truth of culture: a small minority ruling over and exploiting the majority. But it's not the whole truth; it's just the *outward* truth, because while the ruling minority often uses force, in the long run force is not enough. In order to "cook the broth", they've got to get the majority *to accept its exploitation voluntarily.* "This is only possible", says social critic Eric Fromm, "if its mind has been filled with all sorts of lies and fictions, justifying and explaining its acceptance of the minority's rule."*

"For God and King!", "My country right or wrong!": what we've got in our heads, culturally speaking, is a whole lot of stuff that's been made up. Somebody made it up and we bought into it. For instance, we accept that Betty Windsor is a queen—so we treat her like a queen. She gets more and better housing, more and better food; she has rank and wealth and privilege; she never has to worry about a baby-sitter or look for a parking space; and she never has to wait to see the doctor. We go along with all this because we haven't seen through it. It's like the emperor's new clothes. Of course, she believes it too, so she *acts* like a queen. She dresses the part, she doesn't show up at the beach in a bikini, and she doesn't go to the movies. It's fiction and delusion. "Fabrication on a social scale", is the way Eric Fromm describes it—culture carrying us along, telling us what to do and who is to do it.

How is it possible to so captivate a mind, to fill it with fiction and delusion? Why is it so easy to "spell"? Where are the majority while the broth is being cooked! Why are we not watching to keep the pot from boiling! Because we're too busy gathering wood for the fire—and stoking it in the hope that we will get a taste of the broth! In short, we *want* the pot to boil; we want to be fed fiction and delusion. Not only that, we work very hard to feast on this gobbledygook. Make no mistake about it: we don't think we're being spoon-fed; we don't think we're the *object* of someone else's agenda. Just the opposite: we think we're the *subject*; we think we're carving out our own destiny.

"Prisoner, tell me, who was it that wrought this unbreakable chain?" "It was I," said the prisoner, who forged this chain very carefully. I thought my invincible power would hold the world captive leaving me in a freedom undisturbed. Thus night and day I worked at the chain with huge fires and cruel hard strokes. When at last the work was done and the links were complete and unbreakable, I found that it held me in its grip."**

Bengali poet Rabindranath Tagore.

We don't think we're the object of someone else's agenda.... We think we're carving out our own destiny.

In seeking to be masters of our own destiny—to be the *subject* rather than the *object*—we unwittingly seek *subjection*. We are prisoners, forging our own chains. It is a tendency we have seen in the thirty "Recipes" of this Cookbook. Subject to subjection, serve to servitude, mission to submission, bond to bondage...: in order to have the semblance of the one, we are willing to tolerate the despotism of the other. We buy into visions of superiority such as the "pure Aryan race" of Hitler's Germany. We assume the right to be policeman of the world, like the Americans in Kuwait and Vietnam. We cherish an invitation to one of "the Queen's" garden parties, or think ourselves special if we get an audience with "the Pope". We identify with "our" teams who do battle "for us" for a Stanley Cup, a World Cup, a World Series. We gravitate to those who win an Oscar, a Tony or a Grammy in an attempt to forge them into some aspect of ourselves.

And what happens when the bubble bursts, when "Prince" Charles acts less than princely, when Michael Jackson is found to be less than heroic, when O.J. Simpson falls from his teetering pedestal? Do we finally question our subjection, and start coming to terms with ourselves? No. We feed on their demise while we search for someone else to take their places. Anything to keep the pot boiling.

In seeking...to be the subject...we unwittingly seek subjection.

The chiefs in early Fiji enjoyed unlimited power, and subjected their people to the horrors of cannibalism, human sacrifice, widow strangling, female infanticide.... Why did the Fijian people allow this to happen? An anthropologist by the name of A.M. Hocart came to the conclusion that they willingly subjected themselves to their chiefs because they needed a god to be present, a god in the form of someone they could see and talk to. So the chief became their god, and that, says Hocart, "is the true reason for a chief's existence".***

Why do we subject ourselves to kings and queens and princes and princesses? Why do we give slavish devotion to authority figures, some of whom turn out to be tyrannical madmen? Why do we follow with undaunted interest the lives of the rich and famous? Shower adoration on film stars and sports heroes? Offer such reverence and obedience to popes and self-styled gurus? In short, why do we subject ourselves to the socially powerful? Because we, too, want a god-substitute present.

We haven't come to terms with ourselves! We project our unfulfilled "needs" and desires onto outward figures. The monarch, the magnate, the film star, the sports hero, the

religious leader: all become the perfect receptacles for repressed feelings about our own inadequacies.

This is the *inward* truth of culture: the voluntary acceptance of exploitation and distortion. We fill our minds with
fiction and delusion, thereby manufacturing "false consciousness", the secret ingredient in cannibal cookery. No one is
watching to keep the pot from boiling.

A WORD ABOUT SUBSTITUTIONS

The *outward* truth: a small minority ruling over and exploiting the majority. Jail-keepers. The *inward* truth: the voluntary acceptance of exploitation and distortion. Prisoners in love with their chains. These are the truths of culture.

But they're not the whole truth. Why would anyone fall in love with his chains? What are we wanting to lock inside ourselves? What are we trying to keep under wraps? There is something deeper, something going on beneath the surface. As with an iceberg, the part that is submerged is much bigger and more dangerous than the part you can see. That submerged (unconscious) part is the *hidden* truth of culture.

To find the hidden truth we must "come to terms" with ourselves. Who are we, anyway? Well, we are a human species, called *homo sapiens*. *Homo* means "man"; *sapiens* means "wise". *Homo sapiens* is a wise man!

But is that who we are? Or is the term *homo sapiens* part of the "spell"? First of all, we're not all men, and secondly, we're not all wise. And a rose by any other name is still a rose: "humankind" is not so human and not so kind.

Not that we couldn't strive to be. Come to think of it, perhaps a brand new label would give us a new frame of mind.

Something like *hetero sanctum*, maybe; *hetero* being gender-neutral, *sanctum* meaning "holy"—not holy as "religious" in the sense of belief or dogma or ritual, but holy as in being sensitive to life. To the *hetero sanctum* ("holy one"), "survival of the fittest" would not mean "most fit to dominate", but rather, "most fit to coexist".

**Is the term homo sapiens *part of the "spell"?*
*First of all, we're not all men, and secondly,
we're not all wise.***

Before redefining *who* we are, however, we need to come to terms with *what* we are. We are a species of animal, and what we share in common with other animals is that we are tubes. The thing about a tube is that you put stuff in one end and let it out the other.

That's the name of the game. We have to keep putting stuff in and letting it out, otherwise we die—even though, sooner or later, we're going to die anyway. In fact, that very activity is going to wear us out, so the only way you can win at the survival game is to make new tubes. Then the new tubes will repeat the exercise and keep the game going. What makes this stuff so hard to swallow is that all this putting in and letting out is really for the survival of the *species*, not our *selves*. Parents sacrifice for their children like salmon beating their way upstream to spawn. *Culture* tells us to *produce* and *nature* tells us to *reproduce*.

It's a cosmic joke in very bad taste—a litany of living, breathing, feeling human beings making a brief stage appearance in an orchestrated drama where the script is pre-written and the score is prearranged. Put bluntly: first you get a life sentence and then you get a death sentence.

What it boils down to is this: life is just for the time being, for the human being is a *time* being, a creature that lives itself out within the context of history. That makes for a rather unhappy situation because, as the philosopher Plotinus points out, we are poised midway between the beasts and the gods. The beasts are mortal but don't know it. The gods are immortal and do know it. But the poor human being, no longer a beast and not yet a god, is in the worst possible predicament: mortal and knowing it. And the more we have evolved over the millennia, the more conscious we have become of our fate. I am dying—and you are dying, too.

First you get a life sentence, and then you get a death sentence.

Ernest Becker, in his book, *The Denial of Death,* * says consciousness of death, not sex, is the primary repression. We are doomed to die—and we know it—so we spend a good part of our life consciously or unconsciously trying to deny it. The *Bhagavad-Gita*—the Hindu Scriptures—puts it in the form of a question: "Of all the wonders of the world, which is the most wonderful?" The answer is: "That a man, seeing others die around him, still believes he will not die." We have this overriding sense of immortality.

One form of death denial is to identify ourselves with people who are "larger than life" in the hope that their "cosmic significance" will rub off on us. We defer to queens and presidents, priests and popes, film stars and sports heroes in an attempt to immortalize our own *personae.* Another form is to acquire wealth, fame, power, knowledge...things that will imbue us with cosmic significance in our own right.

Symbols of immortality promise to deliver us from the fate of the beasts, and elevate us to the destiny of the "gods". As Becker puts it, we erect cultural symbols which do not age or decay, to quiet our fear of our ultimate end. In this way, cultural activity, the antidote for the terror of death, shows up in the form of "immortality projects"—which leads Ernest Becker to conclude that "culture is a lie about the possibility of victory over death".

I think it's not so much a *lie* as it is a *substitute activity.* Rather than "having our life and having it abundantly", we busy ourselves with projects that will live on after we are gone. Substitute activity is the hidden truth of culture—the denial of death, and its emergence in the form of immortality projects. Simply put, *culture is what a separate self does with death.* And that's the word about substitutions.

DON'T FORGET THE CENTREPIECE

The *outward* truth: a small minority ruling over and exploiting the majority. The *inward* truth: the voluntary acceptance of exploitation and distortion. The *hidden* truth: the denial of death and its emergence in the form of substitute activities. These are the truths of culture. But there is one more truth, the *forgotten* truth. While the hidden truth is about *death*, the forgotten truth is about *life*.

Life is evolution and evolution is transcendence. That is to say, with regard to our own species, the development of the psyche has the same goal as natural evolution: the production of ever higher "unities". In other words, as psychologist Ken Wilber skillfully argues, if the human species in the long process of evolution developed from amoebas, then we are in that same long process developing towards God.* Now that's a very bright future, and it would appear we are now somewhere around the halfway mark.

Perhaps I should clarify what I mean by God, because this is not an attempt to prove the existence of God. I am just saying what outstanding theologians, philosophers, scientists and sages have been saying all along: the existence of God is no more improbable than the existence of matter, energy, nature or cosmos. It's just a matter of what you want to call it: Nature, Energy, Spirit, Consciousness, The Tao, the Atman, God.... In other words, it matters not whether we say all things are forms of Energy, forms of Nature, or forms of God. The point is that this Reality or Suchness or Ground of Being is *One, Whole and Undivided.*

This is what we really are: One, Whole and Undivided. The reason we strive toward cosmic significance is that deep down inside we *intuit* it. By intuit, I mean not to know in the sense of being able to think your way through it, but a gut feeling, a kind of deeper knowing, something *prior*. The closest we come to it is when people have a near-death experience and they tell us, "Oh, yes, now I remember. I've been here before." Invariably they are not overly excited about returning to "the land of the living".

The forgotten truth is that we *are* the centre of the universe. We *are* eternal. We *are* unity. We have just *forgotten* it, forgotten because of the "spell". Our *unity* consciousness has been overshadowed by our *false* consciousness.

The separate self is an illusion—and *culture* is what a *separate* self does with *death.* Culture is a substitute for the dying to (or letting go of) the separate self that would lead us to discover that *nature* is what a *unified* self does with *life*. Until we awaken to that Unity, we will remain spellbound in our separateness.

Our unity consciousness has been overshadowed by our false consciousness.

The Unified Self is the centrepiece in a spaceless and timeless universe. Liberation means a direct and immediate apprehension of this spaceless and timeless Ground of Being. But it takes a lot of "dying" (letting go) to get to that level of living (Being)—and "dying" is not what we do best. So we "forget" death, and in the process, we "forget" our Selves. We forget the centrepiece.

PART IV

ENTERTAINING
IDEAS

SHADOW BOXING

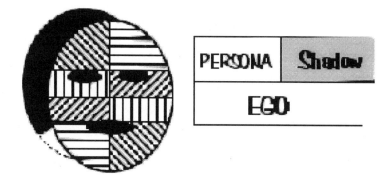

Recipes are formulae for compounding things, for mixing and stirring things up. Since birth we have been compounded by an overwhelming array of influences to the point that our true identity is deeply buried and we have almost completely forgotten it. What remains is a mixture of dissatisfaction, of longing—a vague "knowing" somewhere inside ourselves that we are bound and not free.

It is time to entertain some new ideas in order to get ourselves "out of bounds" because the boundaries we construct and maintain limit our perceptions and create problems. Instead of trying to *solve problems* created by boundaries, we could *dissolve* the *boundaries* that create the problems in the first place.*

The boundaries we construct...limit our perceptions and create problems.

Getting "out of bounds" is an uncovering process, a "demasking" of our culturally constructed *"dividual"*. The process is a journey of expansion inside the mind. Put simply, we need to "re-mind" our *divided* selves in order to "re-member" the *in-dividual* we really are.

We have witnessed the role of culture in formulating the *persona*, and we have seen that, fundamentally, the persona is nothing real. Indeed, it derives its name from the mask an actor wore in Greek drama to indicate the role he was playing.

One of the results of this "cultural role-playing" is a deep sense of separation between the self and the outside world, a world that is perceived as hostile and threatening. When we, as human beings, are bound in the persona, we buy into the hostility while denying the tendency in ourselves. In other words, our tendency toward hostility does not leave us; we just deny that we have it and locate its source in someone or something else. "The world is a dangerous place, and it's getting more dangerous every day."

Our hostility is "not-self" or outside the self, and that which is projected outside the self becomes the *shadow*. Because we identify only with the persona, we carry on a battle with the shadow: "The world is a dangerous place...". As the battle rages, the self shrinks smaller and smaller while the non-self looms larger and larger: "...and it's getting more dangerous every day."

In short, if we live in the persona we shrink the range of our world to protect ourselves from imagined threat. Two essential ingredients are at play: first, we feel the lack of this tendency in ourselves, and secondly, it appears to be "out there". In other words, we project our attack outward, and imagine people attacking us.

Shadow boxing!

Once we "re-own" our shadow, we recognize that, like us, others are just trying to make their lives work.

The first step in de-masking the persona is to get in touch with our feelings. Rather than deny our own sense of hostility, we allow ourselves to feel it. At this initial stage, we do not yet know we are attacking ourselves with our own feelings. We simply perceive attack, and respond by feeling hostile. The attack is still felt to be coming from somewhere else, so we find something or someone else to "hang it on": the Jews, the Christians, the boss, the government, the wife, the dog.... Anyone or anything unlucky enough to put us in touch with our hostility becomes the perfect "hook". In our minds, that someone or something "out there" is the problem, the thing that is "making" us hostile.

The first step in de-masking the persona is to get in touch with our feelings.

It is an interesting paradox: we are attacking someone or something because we are afraid they will attack us. Our fear of *losing* control causes us to *relinquish* control simply by giving "them" power over our feelings: "You make me mad," "You hurt me," "You broke my heart." At least it's a first step: we acknowledge having the feelings.

The second step in the de-masking process is to assume responsibility for our feelings and our states of mind, to realize that the battle between *self* and *other* is really a battle between our *persona* and our *shadow*. People and events "out there" do not cause our hostility. They are merely the occasions for us to feel the hostility we are creating in ourselves.

The third step in de-masking the persona is to "make a translation", to re-read the situation in order to recognize that the thing creating our hostility is our own underlying *fear*. When this translation is first realized, there is a strong tendency to deny it, to pretend that it is not there: "I'm not afraid," "Nothing scares me." Rather than resisting the feeling, however, the idea is to do just the opposite: make room for it, give it "space", befriend it, even encourage it. By accepting the feeling of fear (which is underneath the hostility) we "disappear" the shadow. In so doing, we literally "get our head together", for *persona plus shadow equals ego*. In other words, by getting our head together, we have shifted from living in the *persona* to responding at the level of the *ego*.

People and events "out there" do not cause our hostility. They are merely the occasions for us to feel the hostility we are creating in ourselves.

A healthy ego does not perceive imagined threat from the outside world. It is not spellbound by fear for its basic survival. Once we "re-own" our shadow, we recognize that, like us, others are just trying to make their lives work. While some of us are more skillful at it than others, we are all doing the best we can. With this realization, "outsiders" no longer pose an ever-looming threat. And because we understand our own feelings, we get insight into the dramas others are playing out. When we see hostility, we know there is a frightened persona out there (in there) trying to preserve itself.

Shifting from the *persona* to the *ego* is the first stage in getting "out of bounds."

BODY LANGAUGE

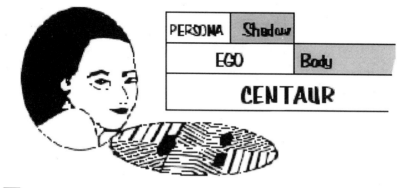

To be bound in the *persona* is to have lost one's mind. To be bound in the *ego* is to have lost one's body. For many of us the body is something that just sort of dangles from the neck. It is our languaging that "spells it out". We say, "I *am* a person", but "I *have* a body".

The split between mind and body is built into the language we use to talk about voluntary versus involuntary functions. The ego controls the voluntary part, our willed thoughts and actions, while the body handles involuntary processes like breathing, circulation and metabolism. Once again, it is our "spelling" that defines the split: "I eat my food", but not "I digest my food." "I move my arm", but not "I beat my heart".

Body language!

Our consciousness is *mind* consciousness, and our bodies are reduced to *property*. As with the shadow, the body becomes an object of projection, something outside our "selves" which we feed, clean, attend to.... It's like a rider who is close to his horse but not *one* with it. When our bodies are well-behaved, we ignore them; when they are unruly, we beat them into submission.* The result is "dis-ease".

What are the reasons for "abandoning" our bodies? At the most superficial level, we feel that the body is "much ado about nothing". It is so obviously there and functions so automatically that we neglect to keep it in awareness. At a deeper level, the body houses strong drives and emotions that are socially taboo. We learn at an early age about "the sins of the flesh". Indeed, the terms "sin" and "flesh" have become almost synonymous in our culture. But at the deepest level, our bodies are the vehicles by which we experience *tension, illness, suffering,* and eventually, *death.*

When our bodies are well-behaved, we ignore them; when they are unruly, we beat them into submission.

Tension. Our first impulse when we feel tension is to "try to relax": "I need a drink", "I need a cigarette", "I need a valium". No matter how hard we try to relax, however, the tension doesn't go away. Indeed, the very process of trying makes us more tense. Instead of trying to force relaxation—with or without the use of chemical aids—the first step is to do just the opposite: notice where the tension is located; get in touch with it, *feel* it.

The second step is to *increase* that tension in order to become *consciously* aware of what we have up to now been doing *unconsciously*: "What am I doing to make myself tense?" Through this process, we take responsibility for our tension and realize we are doing it to ourselves.

The third step is once again to "make a translation", to recognize that every block or tension in the body is a "muscular holding-in" of some impulse that we have not allowed ourselves to express. When this translation is first realized there is a strong tendency to resist it, but rather than resisting the feeling, the idea is, again, to do just the opposite: make room for it; befriend it; encourage it; cry, scream, shout—or beat on a few pillows—in a safe environment. By expressing the pent-up feeling (which is underneath the tension), we "disappear" the boundary between the ego and the projected body.

Illness. A similar process is involved in dealing with illness. The first impulse when we feel "dis-ease" is to eliminate the symptoms. Got a headache? Take an Advil, an Excedrin or a Tylenol. Got a cough? Grab some Benylin or Robitussin. Upset stomach? A Rolaids or a Tums.

The symptoms, however, are attempts on the part of the body to regain its equilibrium. Instead of trying to squelch the symptoms, the first step is to do just the opposite: get in touch with them, feel them, notice where the symptoms are and what they are doing in the body. The second step is to assume responsibility for having them, to realize we are creating dis-ease in ourselves.

The third step is to "make a translation", to re-read the situation in order to recognize the thing that is creating our dis-ease is our own mistreatment of the body. "Translate" this one, for example. It's a recent advertising campaign for a chemical product. A billboard ad displays a hot dog—consisting of a (processed white flour) bun, a weiner (which is made from slaughterhouse scraps such as lips and ears), loaded with mustard, relish and ketchup (complete with preservatives and sugar)—with the following slogan: "You don't have to abstain. Just use protection." Our eye is then drawn to a picture of a roll of Maalox! Another of their billboard ads displays their product next to a giant hamburger, piled higher and thicker than a "Nothing else will Yabba-Dabba Doo! Barney Rubble Bacon Double" with the slogan: "The ones you love always end up hurting you."

When a translation is first realized, there is a strong tendency to deny it, to feel that dis-ease is not something we are doing to our bodies, but something our bodies, by their aging and dying nature, are doing to us. Rather than resisting the source of the discomfort, however, the idea is to embrace it: "What are we doing to make ourselves sick?" When we have asked this question, we have begun the process of changing the way we treat our bodies. By altering the treatment (which is underneath the dis-ease), we again "disappear" a boundary between the ego and the projected body.

Suffering. Re-minding the body—"em-bodying the mind"— is to embrace the human journey, a journey that inevitably leads to suffering. Ken Wilber sums it all up in a few short questions:

> Once you have developed an accurate and healthy ego, what then? Once you have met your egoic goals, once you have

the car and house and some self-esteem, once you have accumulated material goods and professional recognition—once all of that, what then? When history runs out of meaning for the soul, when material pursuits in the outer world go flat in their appeal, when it dawns on you for certain that death alone awaits you, what then?**

It is a new and uncomfortable feeling, and once again the tendency is to resist it. However, the idea is not to resist but to befriend. To make room for it, even encourage this growing dissatisfaction with life. It is not a sign of mental illness and it is not a sign of poor social adjustment—in spite of the fact that psychotherapies, for the most part, aim at "readjustment", undermining the opportunity for people to expand their horizons. (It should not come as a surprise, in this regard, that psychiatrists are commonly referred to as "shrinks".)

"Once you have the car and house and some self-esteem, once you have accumulated material goods and professional recognition—once all of that, what then?"

Dissatisfaction with life is the birth of a growing intelligence which has been buried under the weight of social sham. Suffering, says Wilber, is not so much *good* as it is *a good sign.*

Suffering smashes to pieces complacency of our normal fictions about reality, and forces us to become alive in a special sense—to see carefully, to feel deeply, to touch ourselves and our worlds in ways we have heretofore avoided. It has been said, and truly I think, that suffering is the first grace.***

This awakened intelligence goes well beyond egoic awareness. It recognizes that meaning is found not in outward possessions but in inner being. It is not about *having* much but rather, about *being* much. Life generates both joy and suffering, and this is more than, and different from, the effort to experience pleasure and to avoid pain. Concerns about pleasure and pain, like gain and loss, fame and disgrace, praise and blame, add up to "the unexamined life".

*Death.*The reasons for "abandoning" our bodies are tension, illness, suffering and finally death. As we have discovered, death is our ultimate fear and the true source of anxiety. Indeed, because of our fear of death, anxiety is not something we *have;* it is something we *are.*

The tendency is, once again, to deny, to convert anxiety over death into substitute activities that promise immortality. ("Culture is what a separate self does with death.") The first step in overcoming death anxiety is to do just the opposite: get in touch with it, feel it, make room for it. Secondly, assume responsibility for having (or being) it, then make a translation: "The cause of my anxiety is my fear of impermanence."

Finally, embrace impermanence itself, for impermanence is the natural condition of all living things. Impermanence is not death; it is change. The opposite of death is not life; it is birth. By accepting impermanence (which is underneath the anxiety), we can "disappear" the final boundary between the ego and the body. ("Nature is what a Unified Self does with life.")

Concerns about pleasure and pain, like gain and loss, fame and disgrace, praise and blame, add up to "the unexamined life".

To heal the split between mind and body is to shift from *ego* to *centaur,* a name that derived from that creature in Greek mythology which was half man, half horse, symbolizing the integration of body and mind as a singular unity: the rider, one with his horse. This is not to say the physical body is more profound than the ego, but that the *integration* of body and ego is more profound than either alone.

By being in touch with our bodies, by taking responsibility for our health and well-being, and by embracing the human journey, we can break the "spell" of body language and reach the second stage in getting "out of bounds".

SMOKE AND MIRRORS

PERSONA	Shadow		
EGO		Body	
CENTAUR			Environment
TOTAL ORGANISM			

Persona plus shadow equals ego. Ego plus body equals centaur. Is centaur then the crowning achievement for the more than five billion of us living on a single planet? No, it is the vehicle that delivers us to the edge of another boundary, a boundary that is right on our own doorstep.

Through the lens of a camera aboard a spacecraft on its journey to the moon, we saw ourselves as an organism in space for the very first time.

We have come a long way on our evolutionary journey, but in the whole history of human existence, the most extraordinary event has happened in our own century. Through the lens of a camera aboard a spacecraft on its journey to the moon, we saw ourselves as an *organism in space* for the very first time: patterns of clouds and oceans, green expanses, red and brown soils—and a million species, breathing in, breathing out. One total organism floating within the dark vast sea of the universe. It was an "earth-shattering" discovery because it "brought home" a remarkable realization: we are not born *into* the world; we are born *out of* it. We *are* the world.

The search for life in the universe has led us to ourselves—and none too soon, for we are destroying that life. We are turning productive land into worthless desert. We are cutting down our last remaining rain forests. We are burning fossil fuels, releasing carbon dioxide into the atmosphere, causing global warming. Our industrial gases are depleting the planet's protective ozone shield, accelerating the growth of cancers in humans and other living things. Industrial smokestacks are creating acid rain, killing trees and lakes. Agribusiness is pouring toxic substances into the human food chain and into groundwater....

The camera does not lie. Our self-portrait is not a pretty picture: brown smog, tree stumps, foaming rivers, chemical cesspools, nuclear clouds....

The planet is going up in smoke!

The search for life in the universe has led us to ourselves—and none too soon, for we are destroying that life.

Our environmental threats are human caused and can be traced to our collective mind set. The state of the world is an expression of our fears, illusions and defences "writ large". Our outer world reflects our inner conditions.

The earth is our mirror!

We have seen this symptom before, at the level of the persona where we projected the shadow, at the level of the ego where we projected the body, and now at the level of the *centaur*, where we project the *environment*. The planet is reduced to an object of projection "out there." Earth, air, fire, water: the natural elements become the "enemy" from which we must defend ourselves!

And the "defences" are in place. We manufacture and consume vitamin and mineral supplements to protect ourselves from deficiencies caused by robbing nutrients from the soil. We put energy-consuming air conditioners into our homes,

cars and offices to purify the air and filter out pollutants we
have dumped into the atmosphere. We slap on sunscreens
to protect ourselves from ultraviolet rays intensified by chemicals that deplete the ozone. We purify and filter our drinking
water while we continue to dump toxic waste into the water
supply, and eliminate nature's own filter by stripping water-
sheds of their forests.

> *Our environmental threats are human
> caused and can be traced to our collective
> mind set.*

How do we heal the environment? The task is, again, to
re-own that projected portion of ourselves in order to collapse a boundary. *Centaur* plus *environment* equals *total organism.* "Out there", once again, turns out to be "in here".

We are Earth, a living organism in the midst of many
frozen, silent planets. Unless we awaken to that mystery,
unless we realize that what we do to the Earth we do to ourselves, we will go on deluding with smoke and mirrors until
we, too, become a cold and lifeless world.*

THE DISAPPEARING ACT

UNITY CONSCIOUSNESS

By re-owning the projected environment, we shift from centaur to total organism and we achieve the third stage in getting "out of bounds". Now we recognize that we are One: one with everything on a living planet, mysteriously suspended in time and space.

However, as quantum physics shows, time and space are in themselves illusory boundaries. Einstein's brilliant theory of relativity reveals that linear time—and everything happening within it—is, at best, superficial.

The truth of the "matter" is that the physical world is not composed of matter at all: it is energy and information.

Through our allegiance to culture as a blueprint for survival, we have bought into assumptions which ground us in an objective material world where time exists as an absolute. We perceive the human body, like the environment which nurtures it, as being composed of clumps of matter, and we explain this material world in terms of science: chemical elements, physical laws, biological functions....

The truth of the "matter" is that the physical world is not composed of matter at all: it is energy and information. We are not bounded by space; our perception of *space* is a product of how we have learned to perceive *continuity*. Nor are we the victims of time; our perception of *time* is a product of how we have learned to perceive *change*.

"Our voyage does not begin or end in the physical world," writes Deepak Chopra in *Ageless Body, Timeless Mind*. "However long we stay here to drink the pure water and breathe the life-giving air, eternity is more truly our home."*

Deep inside us, unknown to the five senses, is an innermost core of being, a field of non-change, that creates persona, ego, centaur, organism. These are aspects—but not the totality—of what we are. The goal is not to eliminate these aspects of ourselves, but to eliminate the boundaries between them, for our bodies are part of a universal Body, our minds an aspect of a universal Mind.

How, then, do we become a Unified Being? We cannot *become* it because we already *are* it. We just need to "remember". It is not something to be *done;* it is something to be *seen*—and what is to be seen is the process by which we go about *avoiding* it.

Resisting, clinging and ignoring: these are the three ways we avoid higher levels of consciousness; resisting what is *at* the boundary, clinging to what is *inside* the boundary and ignoring what is *outside* the boundary.

Our bodies are part of a universal Body, our minds an aspect of a universal Mind.

Boundary formation, says Ken Wilber, is the ultimate metaphysical secret. There are no boundaries in Nature. Boundaries are illusions, products not of reality but of the way we map that reality, "And while it is fine to map out the territory, it is fatal to confuse the two."**

This no-boundary reality is the final liberation, the final release, enlightenment, awareness, awakening...; it is Unity Consciousness, the ultimate "disappearing act", the final stage of being out of bounds.

PART V

THE DINNER PARTY

TABLE MANNERS

Life is a veritable feast, a sumptuous buffet of taste, colour, texture and variety, mysterious beyond understanding and imagination. What possibly could be the recipe for a breath of air, a drop of water or a grain of sand; for a blade of grass, a flower or a strawberry; a butterfly, a puppy; for laughter, for music, for love.... The extraordinary thing is that there should be anything happening at all!

More extraordinary still is that we should be here to experience it! Human existence is a cosmic dinner party that is just too marvellous for words! But "man is language", and the cultural spell has turned the dinner party into a cannibal feed. Culture plays on our desires and defences, our fears and fantasies, then further functions to distract, trivialize, and deny. It conspires against the growth of consciousness, dulling us not only to awareness of our own spiritual essence, but to contemplation on the state of the world as well.

Inside each of us is a cannibal trying to get out.

If we are to savour life's cuisine, we need to "re-move" the spell, to "move" from *survive* to *alive*, from "enduring... for many a long day" to being vital, alert, mindful and vigilant—to look, to notice, to *see*. Aliveness is the essence of human existence, the very condition for mental health, which is the same for all people of all ages and in all cultures. "Mental health," writes Eric Fromm,

> is characterized by the ability to love and to create, by the emergence from incestuous ties to clan and soil, by a sense of identity based on one's experience of self as subject and agent of one's powers.*

Why then are so few people "alive" much of the time? Because culture is a blueprint for *survival*, not a blueprint for *aliveness*. In fact, culture actively thwarts aliveness by denying the goals of humanity in the interests of the smaller group.

Will life be a dinner party or a cannibal feed? Will we feast with or on each other?

To move from survival to aliveness is to discover the difference between *understanding* and *wisdom*. The beginning of understanding is to be able to distinguish one thing from another; the beginning of wisdom is to realize there is no distinction, one thing from another.

Good/bad, right/wrong...survival! It is the world of opposites—and the world of opposites is the world of conflict.

Beyond good/bad, beyond right/wrong...aliveness! It is the unity of opposites—"and when the opposites are realized to be one," writes Wilber,

> discord melts into concord, battles become dances, and old enemies become lovers. We are then in a position to make friends with all of our universe, and not just one half of it.**

Aliveness spells an end to cannibal cookery, for while there are cannibals out there, we now know that "out there" is "in here". Inside each of us is a cannibal trying to get out, a cannibal committed to survival at the expense of aliveness, protected by the boundaries we construct around ourselves.

To eliminate boundaries is to eliminate cannibalism, to relieve human suffering in the world and to relieve the causes—beginning with ourselves—that create the suffering in the first place.

Will life be a dinner party or a cannibal feed? Will we feast *with* or *on* each other? Toast the abundance, or carve up the spoils of the kill? The difference is "spelled out" in a few simple...

TABLE MANNERS

Pass the food around; there's plenty.

Don't take more than your share.

Don't start eating until everyone is served.

If you want something, ask for it; don't grab.

Eat what you take; don't waste.

Keep your elbows off the table.

Don't point your fork.

Don't lick your knife.

Don't talk with your mouth full.

Don't belch.

Clean up after yourself.

Remember to give thanks.

These "table manners" are for people who have a very different idea about what it means to be human, manners that would have allowed even those "savage" Fijians and "civilized" Englishmen to dine together comfortably.

And that brings me back to where I started, at the mutiny on the *Bounty*, for the end is also mysteriously the beginning—but with a difference.

To spell an end to cannibalism is, at the same time, to spell an end to the mutiny on the Bounty: mutiny, not a rebellion by a few weary sailors against an unyielding captain, but a greedy and ill-mannered raid on Nature's pantry; and Bounty, not the name of a vessel used to transport breadfruit as cheap food for slaves in the expansion of a colonial empire, but bounty as cornucopia, the vessel of plenty, the joyful feast of life—to which we have all been invited.

Bon appetit!

SAYING GRACE

 Human delicacy
is food for thought.
Let us **not** prey....

May we ever be aware of our own feelings,
   recognizing that when we react
with anger or opposition
   we are struggling against ourselves.

May we listen to our body's wisdom
   and respond to its signals
of tension and disease
   so that we may heal ourselves.

May we remember that the world "out there"
   is a reflection of our reality "in here",
and that what we do to the planet
   we do to ourselves.

May we take time to be silent,
   to reflect and commune with Nature,
aware that we are entering
   into our essential Being.

May we grow from survival to aliveness
   and from understanding to wisdom,
realizing the unity of opposites.
   May we live in the eternal present.

NOTES

CANNIBALISM YESTERDAY AND TODAY

p.18 *Henderson's book is called *Fiji and the Fijians: 1835-1856*, published by Angus & Robertson Ltd. of Australia in 1931. Henderson also prepared for publication *The Journal of Thomas Williams: Missionary to Fiji 1840-1853, Volumes I and II*, published by Angus & Robertson in 1931.

p.21 **Thomas Williams' book was also called *Fiji and the Fijians*. It was published by Alexander Heylin in London in 1858, and reprinted in 1982 by the Fiji Museum in Suva, Fiji. This quote is from page 205 of the reprinted version.

p.21 ***From Chapter VI, "Manners and Customs" pages 205-212 in the 1982 reprint.

GOING FOR THE JUGULAR

p.47 *For the nonspecialist, R.L. Heilbroner (ed.), *The Essential Adam Smith*, W.W. Norton, New York, 1986: a good source for readings and commentary.

MAKING A KILLING

p.51 *From D. Wildenstein & R. Cogniat, *Gauguin*, Thames and Hudson, 1973. A good account of the artist's life and work (with illustrations).

CUTTING THEM DOWN TO SIZE

p.60 *Yeah, I know. This word pair doesn't quite fit the model—but it's exactly what I want to say.

p. 62 **I'm sure the "Queen Mum" didn't mind in the least. This is a critique of inane journalism, not the behaviour of a prominent lady.

A CUT ABOVE THE REST

p.67 *Look at E. Bott, *Tongan Society at the Time of Captain Cook's Visits*, The Polynesian Society, Wellington, 1982.

TAKING A SLICE OUT OF THEM

p.86 *This idea is from an essay called "The Relations between the Ego and the Unconscious" in *Two Essays on Analytical Psychology*, written by Jung in 1917.

SPARE RIBS

p.129 *The Man Who Planted Trees*, written by Jean Giono, was translated into English by Jean Roberts.

THE FAMILY BARBECUE

p.137 *Dr. Kakar wrote a fascinating book called *The Inner World: A Psycho-analytic Study of Childhood and Society in India*, Oxford University Press, 1978.

p.138 **This quote is from Kakar's book on page 49.

p.139 ***Author of the very wise and famous book *The Prophet* from which the present passage is taken.

THEY'LL JUST DIE LAUGHING

p.151 *Noam Chomsky is a linguist, a philospher and an outspoken social critic. He is the author of a number of books and articles on intellectual history and contemporary issues.

p.153 **Neil Postman, *Amusing Ourselves to Death*, Viking, 1985.

MAKING HEADCHEESE

p.156 *Quoted in Ken Wilber's book *Up From Eden*, Shambhala Press, 1983, page 6.

p.156 **This is not to say, of course, that Buddhists have not engaged in killing; they've done their share of it. What it does say is that the killing has not been sanctioned in the name of the Buddha.

p.159 ***A number of wonderful books such as *Education and the Significance of Life* and *Freedom from the Known* have preserved Krishnamurti's many spontaneous talks. This idea is from the former.

TOO MANY COOKS SPOIL THE BROTH
p.182 *This idea is discussed at length in a book
   called *Zen Buddhism and Psychoanalysis* by Eric
   Fromm, written with D.T. Suzuki and Richard De
   Martino, Harper & Row, 1960.

A WATCHED POT NEVER BOILS
p.184 *Also from Eric Fromm, et al, *Zen Buddhism and
   Psychoanalysis*, page 98.
p.185 **From *Gitanjali* ("Song Offerings"), a collection
   of prose translations made by Tagore from the
   original Bengali, and published by Macmillan &
   Company, London, 1961.
p.186 ***A.M. Hocart, *The Northern States of Fiji*, Royal
   Anthropological Institute, Occasional Paper No.11,
   1952.

A WORD ABOUT SUBSTITUTIONS
p.190 *The Denial of Death*, The Free Press, 1973.

DON'T FORGET THE CENTREPIECE
p.191 *For an in-depth discussion of this idea, look at
   Ken Wilber's brilliant book *Up From Eden*,
   Shambhala Press, 1983.

SHADOW BOXING
p.195 *The inspiration for this framework comes from
   Ken Wilber, *No Boundary: Eastern and Western
   Approaches to Personal Growth*, Shambhala, 1981.

BODY LANGUAGE
p.199 *For a more detailed discussion of the mind/
   body split, I refer the reader to Chapter 8 in *No
   Boundary*.
p.202 **From *No Boundary*, page 119.
p.202 ***From *No Boundary*, page 85.

SMOKE AND MIRRORS

p.206 *Three books which explore these ideas in greater detail are *Our Common Future*, by the World Commission on Environment and Development, Oxford University Press, 1987; Roger Walsh's *Staying Alive: The Psychology of Human Survival*, Shambhala, 1984, and my own previous book *Island in Space: Prospectus for a New Idea*, United Nations, 1986.

THE DISAPPEARING ACT

p.208 *Ageless Body, Timeless Mind*, Harmony Books, 1993, page 315.

p.208 **No Boundary*, page 31.

TABLE MANNERS

p.212 *Eric Fromm in *The Sane Society*, page 58.

p.212 **No Boundary*, page 29.

SELECTED BIBLIOGRAPHY

These four prominent writer/thinkers have illuminated the "remedies" for "human sacrifice":

Fromm, Eric.
  Escape from Freedom, Avon Books, 1941.
  Man for Himself, Fawcett Premier Books, 1947.
  The Sane Society, Fawcett Premier Books, 1955.
  The Art of Loving, Harper & Row, 1956.
  Psychoanalysis and Religion, Vail-Ballou Press, 1950.
  Zen Buddhism and Psychoanalysis, (with D.T. Suzuki & Richard De Martino), Harper & Row, 1960.
Jung, Carl.
  Two Essays on Analytical Psychology, Collected Works, Volume 7.
  The Archetypes of the Collective Unconscious, Collected Works, Volume 9.i.
  Aion: Researches into the Phenomenology of the Self, Collected Works, Volume 9.ii.
Krishnamurti, Jiddu.
  The Awakening of Intelligence, Avion Books, 1973.
  The First and Last Freedom, Harper & Row, 1975.
  Education and the Significance of Life, Harper & Row, 1981.
  Freedom from the Known, Harper & Row, 1983.
  Think on These Things, Krisnamurti Foundation, 1964.
Wilber, Ken.
  The Spectrum of Human Consciousness, Theosophical Publishing House, 1977.
  No Boundary, Shambhala, 1979.
  The Atman Project, Theosophical Publishing, 1980.
  Up from Eden, Shambhala, 1983.
  A Sociable God, Shambhala, 1984.

INSIGHT TEACHINGS©

with Dr. Pamela Peck

insight: *"the capacity to discern the true nature of a situation."*

"Stepping into another culture," says Cultural Anthropologist Dr. Peck, "is the best way to see through your own." And "seeing through your own" is the best way to free yourself from the cultural conditioning that numbs the body, dulls the mind and kills the spirit.

INSIGHT TEACHINGS© are like anthropological fieldtrips to strange and distant cultures. The four programs in the series—Encounter Culture©, Out of Bounds©, Anthrojournal©, and The Quest© (described overleaf)—show us how to "re-view" the world and how to "re-mind" ourselves so that we might more completely enter into the mystery and opportunity of life.

Dr. Peck is also available to speak to educational, professional and service groups.

TREASURES FROM CANNIBAL ISLE©

Place authentic Pacific Island handicrafts on your dinner table and be part of a project that assists local island women's groups and cooperatives to better their social conditions and educate their children. Hand-carved Fijian cannibal forks top the list, alongside such artifacts as hand-made tapa cloth place mats, and napkin rings woven from pandanus leaves. For a complete list of these small treasures with a big purpose, contact the publisher.

For more information on INSIGHT TEACHINGS© or to purchase copies of THE CANNIBAL'S COOKBOOK©, please contact the Publisher by fax at **604 872-5917**, or by mail at:

PJenesis Press,
City Square P.O. Box 47105,
Vancouver, Canada, V5Z 4L6.

Crack the code of culture!

Encounter Culture© is a "hands-on" exploration of the role of culture in the formation of our perceptions about ourselves and the outside world. Applying the methods anthropologists use to understand "rite of passage," participants discover in a dramatic and novel way how these perceptions are formed, and how they are maintained and reinforced. With this insight, they move "underneath" and "through" the deeper structures of culture in order to free themselves from the illusive constraints of the social world.

Where do you draw the line?

OUT OF BOUNDS© takes participants on a lively journey of expanded awareness. In the seminar, we identify, move toward, then break through a series of limiting boundaries. In the process, we gain insight into how boundaries are constructed and maintained, how boundaries limit our perceptions and create problems, and how we all struggle—with varying degrees of success—to solve these problems. When we shift from trying to solve problems to dissolving the boundaries that create the problems in the first place, we discover progressively more "space" within which to "live, move and have our being."

Write the story of your life!

Anthrojournal© is for people who are ready to engage in authentic self-discovery, and who want to critically examine their life goals. Inspired by the methods anthropologists use to analyze and interpret myth, it provides a framework for participants to write the *real* story of their life. In a short period of time, *anthrojournaling* enables them to see—in a way they have not seen before—the path they more or less unwittingly follow. This critical insight creates a new starting point for embarking on the rest of their personal human journey.

Does spirit matter? Or does matter spirit?

The Quest © is a probe into the very essence of what it means to be human. Grounded in the anthropological study of religion, it provides a framework that outlines, then moves beyond the culturally prescribed ways we approach the mysterious. It does not subscribe to a particular viewpoint nor engage in a spiritual discipline. Rather, it investigates a variety of religious experiences, and situates them within a spectrum of human consciousness so that participants can authenticate their own experience.